DK EYEWITNESS

TOP**10**
SAN FRANCISCO

T0104143

Top 10 San Francisco Highlights

The Top 10 of Everything

CONTENTS

San Francisco Area by Area

Streetsmart

Within each Top 10 list in this book, no hierarchy of quality or popularity is implied. All 10 are, in the editor's opinion, of roughly equal merit.

Throughout this book, floors are referred to in accordance with American usage; i.e., the "first floor" is at ground level.

Title page, front cover and spine *The majestic Golden Gate Bridge over the Pacific Ocean*
Back cover, clockwise from top left *The Painted Ladies, Alamo Square; Alcatraz Island; Lombard Street; Oakland Bay Bridge; cable car*

The rapid rate at which the world is changing is constantly keeping the DK Eyewitness team on our toes. While we've worked hard to ensure that this edition of San Francisco is accurate and up-to-date, we know that opening hours alter, standards shift, prices fluctuate, places close and new ones pop up in their stead. So, if you notice we've got something wrong or left something out, we want to hear about it. Please get in touch at **travelguides@dk.com**

Welcome to
San Francisco

The glowing Golden Gate Bridge, spanning the stunning Bay, is the quintessential image of San Francisco, but this vibrant city has so much more to offer – from eclectic architecture to outdoor activities, a gutsy cultural scene to a packed events calendar. With DK Eyewitness Top 10 San Francisco, it's yours to explore.

The misty hills of San Francisco have known Spanish conquistadors, Mexican settlers, the fortune seekers of the Gold Rush, and today's lively Latin American, European, Filipino, Russian, and Pan-Asian populations – each with their own festivals, neighborhoods, and restaurants. This cultural diversity is integral to this town's success – a walk from one neighborhood to another reveals thriving community hubs, full of independent stores celebrating traditions and heritage. And that's not to mention the food scene: the sheer variety of restaurants, from sushi bars to dim sum spots, farm-to-table joints to top-class taquerías, make SF (as the locals know it) a foodie haven.

The city shines with culture, from the **San Francisco Museum of Modern Art (SFMOMA)** and the **de Young Museum** to opera in **Golden Gate Park** and the **Fillmore Jazz Festival**. To intrepid explorers, the city reveals more hidden treasures, from the backstreet **Tin How Temple** to the cypress-tree sculptures in the **Presidio** forest. The city's annual events are legendary: the **Bay to Breakers** race, the explosive **Lunar New Year** parade, and of course the dazzling pageantry of the **San Francisco Pride parade**.

Whether you're visiting for a weekend or a week, our Top 10 guide brings together the best of everything the city has to offer, from iconic sights like **Alcatraz** to day trips to the **Wine Country**. The guide has useful tips throughout, from seeking out what's free to finding the best beaches, plus eight easy-to-follow itineraries, designed to tie together a clutch of sights in a short space of time. Add inspiring photography and detailed maps, and you've got the essential pocket-sized travel companion. **Enjoy the book, and enjoy San Francisco**.

Clockwise from top: **Golden Gate Bridge, street in Chinatown, a cable car, sailing by Alcatraz, Music concourse in Golden Gate Park, sea lions at Pier 39, detail of City Hall's interior**

Exploring San Francisco

From the back alleys of Chinatown to the Pacific shores, San Francisco offers visitors everything from historic sites and museums to cruises in the vast Bay. Here are some ideas for making the most of your stay, whether you have a weekend to fit in the "must sees," or have enough time for day trips and exploring the city's hidden gems.

Vibrant Pagoda at the Japanese Tea Garden.

The Ferry Building has a great gourmet food market.

Two Days in San Francisco

Day ❶
MORNING

Start the day at **Fisherman's Wharf** *(see pp16–17)* where the Eagle Café on the second floor of Pier 39 serves American breakfasts with Bay views. Then take the **Cable Car** *(see pp14–15)* to **Union Square** *(see p89)*, where luxury department stores and boutiques glitter around the historic plaza.

AFTERNOON

Walk a few blocks to **Yerba Buena Gardens** *(see pp34–5)*, a sprawling park and arts hotspot. Highlights include **SFMOMA** *(see pp32–3)* and a state-of-the-art movie theater at **Metreon** *(see p34)*. Just across the street is the **Contemporary Jewish Museum (CJM)** *(see p35)*. End the day with dinner in **Chinatown** *(see pp22–3)*.

Day ❷
MORNING

After a traditional San Francisco breakfast of Dungeness crab omelette and Irish coffee at **The Buena Vista Café** *(see p101)*, take a ferry across the Bay to **Alcatraz** *(see pp18–19)* for a moving tour of the historic prison.

AFTERNOON

Walk or bike across the **Golden Gate Bridge** *(see pp12–13)* and back, then stroll on the shoreline past **Crissy Field** *(see p98)*, **Marina Green** *(see p56)*, **Aquatic Park** *(see p98)*, and the **Maritime National Historical Park** *(see p17)*, followed by a seafood feast at **Scoma's** *(see p101)*.

Four Days in San Francisco

Day ❶
MORNING
In **Golden Gate Park** (see pp24–5), take tea in the Japanese Tea Garden. Nearby is the **de Young Museum** (see pp28–9). Enjoy lunch on the terrace of its sculpture garden.

Key
— Two-day itinerary
— Four-day itinerary

AFTERNOON
Explore the rainforest and the living roof at the **California Academy of Sciences** (see pp26–7), row around **Stow Lake** (see p24), and admire the Dutch Windmill. Have dinner at **Beach Chalet Brewery** (see p123).

Day ❷
MORNING
Learn about early California history at the oldest building in the city, **Mission Dolores** (see p109), before heading to a sidewalk table at **Caffè Trieste** (see p74) in North Beach for a pizza slice, focaccia sandwich, and a cappuccino. Up the street, the spires of **Saints Peter and Paul Church** (see p90) tower over **Washington Square** (see p90), while **Coit Tower** (see p48) has Depression-era murals.

AFTERNOON
Head to **Yerba Buena Gardens** (see pp34–5) and explore **SFMOMA** (see pp32–3) and the other museums, galleries, and gardens. Afterwards, walk to **Chinatown** (see pp22–3) and discover the **Tin How Temple** (see p62). Enjoy the multitude of classic Shanghai dumplings on offer at **Yank Sing** (see p93).

Day ❸
MORNING
Take in the woodlands, vistas, and Civil War sites of **The Presidio** (see p56). Savor a lunch at one of the restaurants in the park.

AFTERNOON
Explore **Fisherman's Wharf** (see pp16–17), being sure not to miss the sea lions at Pier 39. Then take a ferry across the Bay to **Alcatraz** (see pp18–19) for a tour of the prison. End the day with a ride in a **Cable Car** (see pp14–15) to **Union Square** (see p89) for dinner.

Day ❹
MORNING
Cross the **Golden Gate Bridge** (see pp12–13) and drive an hour north to the **Wine Country** (see pp36–9). Visit the Hess Collection to enjoy a winery tour and tasting.

AFTERNOON
Relax in the spas and restaurants of **Yountville** (see p36) before returning to the city and **Nob Hill** (see p87) for cocktails at the **InterContinental Mark Hopkins** (see p145).

Sea lions can often be seen basking in the sun at Pier 39.

Top 10 San Francisco Highlights

The living roof of the California Academy of Sciences

TOP 10 San Francisco Highlights

After a few days of taking in the sights and sounds of San Francisco, many visitors proclaim this city to be their new favorite. The geographical setting evokes so much drama, the light seems clearer, the colors more vivid, the cultural diversity so inviting, that it's a place almost everyone can fall in love with at first sight.

Golden Gate Bridge ①
This symbol of the city is one of the world's largest single span bridges (see pp12–13).

② Cable Cars
These little troopers now form the world's only system of its kind that still plays a daily role in urban life (see pp14–15).

③ Fisherman's Wharf
The views from here are unmatched. You can also see sea lions and try great seafood (see pp16–17).

Alcatraz ④
"The Rock" continues to capture the imagination. The views from the ferry are worth the visit alone (see pp18–21).

Chinatown ⑤
Home to one of the world's largest Chinese communities outside of Asia, this busy neighborhood is a magnet for locals and visitors alike (see pp22–3).

Golden Gate Park ⑥

The city has one of the world's largest public parks, with natural beauty and fine museums *(see pp24–5)*.

⑧ de Young Museum

A cultural landmark housing American, Oceanian, and African art, as well as temporary exhibits *(see pp28–9)*.

⑦ California Academy of Sciences

This site houses a planetarium, aquarium, and natural history museum under one roof *(see pp26–7)*.

⑨ SFMOMA

An architectural landmark of the city, SFMOMA houses digital installations and 20th-century masterworks of painting, sculpture and photography, as well as temporary exhibitions *(see pp32–5)*.

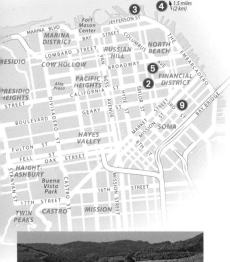

⑩ The Wine Country

This picturesque area of Northern California produces some exceptionally fine wines *(see pp36–9)*.

TOP 10 ⭐ Golden Gate Bridge

As with most of the world's wonders, many said the Golden Gate Bridge could never be built – the span was too wide, the ocean too deep, and the cost too great. In 1872, railroad tycoon Charles Crocker conceived the idea, but it took a visionary engineer, Joseph Strauss, to put forth a realistic proposal in 1921. After 10 years of opposition, funding was finally secured. The bridge opened in 1937, and has been an emblem of San Francisco, and America's icon on the Pacific, ever since.

1 Deco Style
The bridge **(right)** owes its striking style to the consulting architect Irving F. Morrow. He simplified the pedestrian railings to uniform posts placed far enough apart to allow for unobstructed, breathtaking views.

2 Bridge Celebrations
The bridge opened on May 27, 1937, and has been central to the city's soul ever since, the setting for everything from firework celebrations to political demonstrations.

3 Fort Point Lookout
This National Historic Site **(left)** was completed in 1861. It offers soaring views of the underside of the bridge and of the pounding waters of the ocean.

4 Toll System
Since 1937, cars have had to pay a toll to cross the bridge. Now, only city-bound traffic is charged, and in 2013 the system was made fully electronic in order to ease the traffic congestion from stopping at toll booths.

5 Maintenance
Repairing the bridge **(below)** is an ongoing task and it's repainted continuously; the famous "International Orange" paint protects it from the salt in the air.

THE STATISTICS

The length of the steel wires used to make the cables of the bridge is enough to circle the earth three times. It is also brilliantly "over-engineered" and is said to be five times stronger than it needs to be to withstand the winds and tides it endures daily. At the time it was built, it was the longest suspension bridge in the world (it now ranks twelfth) and took just over four years to build. About 40 million vehicles cross the bridge annually, streaming across six lanes of traffic, along its 1.7-mile (2.7-km) length. The bridge is equipped with two foghorns, each with a different pitch, and 360-degree flashing red beacons. The bridge has been closed due to high winds only three times in its history.

⑧ Building the Bridge
Strauss introduced the use of hard hats **(above)** and a safety net that saved 19 workers' lives.

⑨ Cruises
For a unique view of the bridge, take a cruise around the Bay. Options range from sightseeing trips to special tours.

⑩ Marin Vista Point
Crossing over to the north side, pull off just before the end to take in the panorama from the Vista Point. Look back at the hills and spires of the city.

Star Turns in Movies ⑥
The bridge has starred in many movies, most notably Alfred Hitchcock's *Vertigo*, in which James Stewart pulls Kim Novak from the raging surf, just east of Fort Point *(see p98)*. In *A View to a Kill* **(right)**, 007 and Christopher Walken battle it out, both clinging to its aerial heights.

⑦ Hiking and Biking
The bridge is open to walkers and cyclists. Urban hiking trails and cycle routes can be found on both sides of the bridge, in the Presidio and along the Marin Headlands.

NEED TO KNOW
MAP C1
- (415) 921-5858
- www.goldengate.org

- The bridge has an ongoing construction of protective barriers – steel nets that will blend in with the existing infrastructure – to help deter suicide attempts.

- Cruises depart from the Embarcadero Pier and Sausalito. Quality purveyors include Hornblower Cruises *((888) 467-6256; www.cityexperiences.com)* and Call of the Sea/Seaward *((415) 331-3214; www.callofthesea.org)*.

🔟 ⭐ Cable Cars

It's impossible not to love these vestiges of another age, as they valiantly make their way up the precipitous hills. Yet they came perilously close to being scrapped in 1947, when a "progressive" mayor announced it was time for buses to take their place. An outraged citizenry prevailed, and the system was declared a National Historic Landmark in 1964. In the early 1980s, it underwent a $60 million overhaul. The present service of about 40 cars covers some 10 miles (16 km).

1 Bell

While operating up and down the hills, the cable car's bell **(right)** is used by the grip person like a klaxon, to warn other vehicles and pedestrians of imminent stops, starts, and turns.

2 Grip Person

The grip person **(below)** must be quick-thinking and strong to operate the heavy gripping levers and braking mechanisms. The grip acts like a huge pair of pliers that clamp onto the cable to pull the car along.

3 Cars

Cable cars **(right)** come in two types: one that has a turnaround system, one that does not. All of them are numbered, have wood-and-brass fittings in the 19th-century style, and are often painted in differing colors. One car can accommodate around 60 to 70 passengers.

CABLE CARS AND STREETCARS

Andrew Hallidie's cable car system dates from August 2, 1873, when he tested his prototype based on mining cars. It was an immediate success and spawned imitators in more than a dozen cities world-wide. However, 20 years later, it was set to be replaced by the electric streetcar. Fortunately, resistance to above-ground wires, corruption in City Hall, and finally the 1906 earthquake, sidetracked those plans. The cable car was kept for the steepest lines, while the streetcar took over the longer, flatter routes.

4 Conductor

The cable car conductor collects fares, but also makes sure that everyone travels safely, and that the grip person has room to work.

5 Braking

Cable cars have three different brakes. Wheel brakes press against the wheels; track brakes press against the tracks when the grip person pulls a lever; the emergency brake is a steel wedge forced into the rail slot.

6 Riding Styles

There is a choice of sitting inside a glassed-in compartment, sitting outside on wooden benches, or hanging onto poles and standing on the running board. The third option is the best one for enjoying the enticing sights, sounds, and smells of San Francisco.

8 Turntables

Part of the fun of the cable car experience is being there to watch when the grip person and conductor turn their car around for the return trip (above). The best view is at Powell and Market Streets.

9 Cables

The underground cables are 1.25 inches (3 cm) in diameter and consist of six steel strands of 19 wires, wrapped around a shock-absorbing rope.

10 Routes

The three existing routes cover the Financial District, Nob Hill, Chinatown, North Beach, Russian Hill, and Fisherman's Wharf areas. As these are always important destinations for visitors – and for many residents, too – most people will find that a cable car ride is a practical, as well as a pleasurable, experience.

7 Cable Car Museum

Downstairs, look at the giant sheaves (wheels), which keep the cables moving throughout the system (below); upstairs there are displays of some of the earliest cable cars.

NEED TO KNOW

Cable Car Museum: **MAP M3**; 1201 Mason St at Washington; (415) 474-1887; open Apr–Sep: 10am–6pm daily (Oct–Mar: until 5pm); www.cablecarmuseum.org

- Rather than wait in the long lines at a cable car terminus, do what the locals do and walk up a stop or two, where you can hop on right away for a $8 fee – then hold on!

- The $8 fare is for one ride, in one direction, with no transfers. Consider getting a CityPass or a Muni Passport – 1 day for $24, 3 days for $36, and 7 days for $47 (see pp134–5).

🔟⭐ Fisherman's Wharf

Tourists, enjoying takeout crab cocktails and sourdough bread, crowd the sidewalks and souvenir stands of the old seaside wharf district. Amid today's seafood restaurants, aquarium, wax museum, and Bay cruise piers, fishing boats become great photo ops as their catches of Dungeness crab and Pacific fish are unloaded. The rowdy old days of the 1850s are reenacted on masted schooners, while a World War II-era submarine and a Liberty ship recall the city's long history as a major port.

PIER 39 ①
One of the most popular attractions in the city is set on a landscaped pier with dazzling Bay views, restaurants, live entertainment, and shops **(right)**. Get discount coupons at the California Welcome Center. Families love the bungee jump, mirror maze, games arcade, and carousel.

② Ghirardelli Square
The Ghirardelli family used this square *(see p100)* as the head-quarters of the Ghirardelli Chocolate Company from 1895 until 1962. The site is now home to upscale shops and restaurants.

③ Aquarium of the Bay
The transparent tunnel of the aquarium visually immerses you in the San Francisco Bay marine habitat, where thousands of different species of spectacular ocean fauna disport themselves before your eyes. Video presentations and marine specialist guides help you to understand what you're seeing.

Anchorage Square Shopping Center ④
Set in the heart of Fisherman's Wharf, this center **(right)** has plenty of stores, restaurants, and entertainment.

⑤ Boudin Bakery
This is the home of the famous chain of San Francisco sourdough breadmakers **(left)**. Try the crusty round loaf, best enjoyed warm from the oven with plenty of butter.

⑥ Madame Tussauds
Incredibly lifelike wax figures of movie stars, music legends, political and sports icons, and San Francisco celebrities are on display here. A scary "Dungeon" theatrical show is for ages 10 and up.

Fisherman's Wharf

7 The Cannery

Built as a warehouse in 1907, the building underwent a makeover in 1967, and it's now the site of some appealing boutiques, as well as tourist shops.

8 Fish Alley

This alley is possibly the last vestige of the traditional, workaday wharf. Here you can see fishing boats come in and watch as the catch of the day is landed and prepared for market.

9 Maritime National Historical Park

At the Hyde Street Pier **(below)** are vessels ranging from 1880s schooners and a spectacular 1886 square-rigger to 1900s tugs and the USS *Pampanito* World War II submarine.

THE PORT OF SAN FRANCISCO

Born out of the California Gold Rush of 1849, the Port of San Francisco stretches nearly 8 miles (13 km) from the Hyde Street Pier to India Basin. A cruise ship terminal hosts 80 cruise ship calls and 300,000 passengers annually, while freighters lumber under the Golden Gate Bridge and ferries, water taxis, fishing boats, and yachts bustle to and from the Ferry Building, Fisherman's Wharf, and Embarcadero piers and marinas.

10 SS Jeremiah O'Brien Liberty Ship

At Pier 45 floats this restored World War II Liberty ship *(see p62)*. Take a free tour to hear tales of the thousands of troops ferried across the seas.

NEED TO KNOW

Aquarium of the Bay: MAP J4; Embarcadero; (415) 623-5300; open 11am–6pm daily; adm $31.75 adults, $21.75 children, under-3s free; www. aquariumofthebay.org

Anchorage Square Shopping Center: MAP J3; 333 Jefferson St; (415) 775-6000; www.anchorage square.com

Madame Tussauds: MAP J3; 145 Jefferson St; adm fee varies, check website to book in advance: www.madame tussauds.com

Maritime National Historical Park: MAP J1; 499 Jefferson St; open 10am–4pm daily (last entrance 3:30pm); adm $15; under-16s free; www. maritime.org

SS Jeremiah O'Brien Liberty Ship: MAP J3; Pier 45; (415) 544-0100 (call or visit the kiosk site for opening hours; adm $10–$20; under-5s free; www.ssjeremiah obrien.org

■ To sample some of the best seafood in the city, head straight to the culinary stalwart Scoma's *(see p101)*.

⭐ Alcatraz

Alcatraz was one of the US's busiest detention centers during its 29 years in operation. Prisoners of the penitentiary were infamously confined to small cells, where the slow passage of time became psychological torture. It closed in 1963 due to the facility's high upkeep costs. Today, the island is part of the National Park Service and tours here attract thousands of visitors every year.

THE HISTORY OF "THE ROCK"

The name "Alcatraz" derives from the Spanish *alcatraces*, for the sea birds that Spanish explorer Juan Manuel de Ayala observed here when he sailed into the Bay in 1775. In 1850, the island was set aside for the US Army to build a citadel, but defense became less of a priority and, in 1907, it became a military prison. In 1934 the Federal Government opened a maximum-security penitentiary here. Yet Alcatraz was not quite the "Devil's Island" that many think it was – the conditions were better than many other prisons.

1 Chapel

In the 1920s a Mission-style military chapel **(above)** was built above the guardhouse. It was used as living quarters and a school. During the post-1930s phase, it housed prison staff.

2 Tours

Rangers lead guided tours focusing on the Occupation of Alcatraz *(see p21)*, the gardens, birdwatching, and more.

3 Recreation Yard

Good behavior qualified prisoners for a turn around the walled-in recreation yard **(left)**. Here, they could walk outside of their cells, where they spent between 16 and 23 hours a day.

4 Lighthouse

Alcatraz was the site of the first lighthouse **(above)** built on the West Coast in 1854. The original was replaced in 1909 to tower above the new cell block.

5 Control Room

Guards controlled the security system from this bunker-like facility **(above)**. Next to the Control Room was the visiting area, where thick glass separated prisoners and visitors, and conversations were held over telephones.

6 Broadway

The corridor that separates C and B blocks was jokingly nick-named by prisoners after New York City's glittering thoroughfare, famous for its nightlife. The intersection at the end was named "Times Square."

7 Cell Blocks

The cell house contains four free-standing cell blocks **(below)**. The complex was built by military prisoners in 1911 and was once the largest reinforced concrete building in the world. In all, there were 390 cells, but the prison population averaged only about 260 at any one time.

NEED TO KNOW

MAP K5

Alcatraz Cruises (Hornblower) from Pier 33: (415) 981-7625 (tickets and schedules); open daily; adm: day tours: $42.15 adult, $39.80 senior, $25.80 child 5–11 years; night tours: $52.70 adult, $49 senior, $31 child 5–11 years; family packages available; tour compulsory; www.alcatrazcruises.com

■ A picturesque way to reach the island is on a cruise.

■ Picnicking is allowed on the dock, but you'll have to bring your own food.

■ The weather here is blustery and cold, and the trails are rough. Wear warm clothes and comfortable shoes.

■ A cell-house audio tour explores the prison and its stories. Available in 11 languages, it is included in the price of the ticket.

9 Mess Hall

Meals were one of the few things prisoners had to look forward to, and they were generally well fed to quell rebellion. Note the sample menu at the entrance to the kitchen **(below)**.

8 Warden's House

The warden's once-luxurious house **(below)** is now a ruin after burning down in 1970. Designed in Mission Revival style, the home had 17 large rooms, and sweeping views of the Golden Gate Bridge and San Francisco's lights.

10 Building 64

The theater and orientation center are located in the old bar-racks building behind the ferry jetty. The building also houses a bookstore, exhibits, and a multimedia show providing a historical overview of Alcatraz.

Stories from The Rock

Burt Lancaster in *Birdman of Alcatraz*

1 Robert "Birdman" Stroud
The most famous inmate was dubbed the "Birdman of Alcatraz," despite the fact that he was not permitted to conduct his avian studies during his 17 years here. Due to his violent nature and many manslaughter convictions, Stroud spent most of those years in solitary.

2 Birdman of Alcatraz
This 1962 movie presented Robert Stroud as a nature-loving ornithologist, bending historical fact to the service of a good story.

3 Al Capone
In 1934 Capone was among the first "official" shipment of prisoners. The infamous gangster was assigned menial jobs and treated like every other inmate.

4 George "Machine Gun" Kelly
Jailed in 1933 for kidnapping, Kelly was given a life sentence, and was sent to Alcatraz for 17 years of his sentence. He was considered a model prisoner by the officers.

5 Alvin "Creepy" Karpis
Karpis robbed his way through the Midwest between 1931 and 1936, and earned himself the title Public Enemy Number One. He was imprisoned on Alcatraz from 1936 to 1962. He committed suicide in 1979.

6 Morton Sobell
Charged with conspiracy to commit treason by spying for the Soviets, Sobell arrived on Alcatraz in 1952 and spent five years as its most famous political prisoner, being a victim of J. Edgar Hoover's witch hunt for Communist subversives. Once freed, Sobell returned to live in San Francisco for many years.

7 Anglin Brothers
The brothers, John and Clarence, are notable as two of the five known inmates to successfully escape from The Rock.

Clint Eastwood in *Escape from Alcatraz*

8 Escape from Alcatraz
Starring Clint Eastwood as Frank Morris, who escaped along with the Anglin brothers. Again, this 1979 film is largely Hollywood fiction. However, the depiction of prison life is reportedly accurate.

9 Frank Wathernam
The last prisoner to leave Alcatraz, on March 21, 1963.

10 The Rock
Hollywood has never lost its fascination with Alcatraz, as can be seen in this 1996 action thriller, starring Sean Connery.

OCCUPATION OF ALCATRAZ

In 1969 Richard Oakes and 90 members of the Indians of All Tribes activist group landed on Alcatraz, set up camp, and demanded that the government sell them the island for $24 worth of beads and red cloth. They argued that they were entitled to ownership of the island as reparations after a similar-sized island was taken from the community 300 years earlier. The government considered forcibly removing the occupiers, but growing public support for the Native Americans forced officials to renew negotiations. However, in January, 1970, while playing on the rooftop of one of the buildings, Oakes' youngest daughter slipped and fell to her death; distraught, he and his family decided to abandon their claim. Sixty Native Americans remained, but as the stalemate dragged on, the majority slowly began to leave – only 15 chose to stay. In June, 1970, fires ravaged the warden's house, the recreation hall, the officers' club, and the lighthouse. Following this devastation, government troops staged a pre-dawn raid. The remaining Native Americans were arrested and the 19-month occupation came to an end.

The prison garden at Alcatraz Island

TOP 10 HORTICULTURAL GEMS OF ALCATRAZ

1 Mexican Blanket: Find these daisy-like flowers every summer and fall.

2 Roses: The island is home to various types of fragrant rose bushes.

3 Fuchsia: Numerous variants produce delicate, vivid violet flowers.

4 Succulents: Subtropical succulents including agave and aloe thrive under the fog-covered sun.

5 Pelargonium: Also known as geraniums, these flowers come in many bright reds and pinks.

6 Fig trees: Planted by an inmate gardener in the 1940s, these trees draw songbirds to their fruits.

7 Iris: Every spring, dozens of pastel variants of this annual flower spring from the island's sandy ground.

8 Dahlia: Also known as "Yellow Gems" or "Yellow stars", Dahlias are a common sight in the Alcatraz Garden.

9 Sage: Types of this fragrant herb are planted throughout the island.

10 Poppies: California's state flower blooms in numerous colors and variants all over Alcatraz.

A Native American man in complete ceremonial attire as he stands in an open cell in the former Alcatraz Prison during the occupation.

⭐ Chinatown

Considered the oldest Chinatown in the country, this densely populated neighborhood – with its bright facades, lively markets, serene temples, and staple Chinese restaurants and shops – is a place every visit to San Francisco should include. The atmosphere echoes that of a typical southern Chinese town, but with a noticeable American influence sprinkled throughout. Overlook the tourist clichés and speak to locals for the best tips and guidance, giving yourself enough time to take it all in.

Chinatown Gate ❶
A gift from Taiwan in 1970, this triple-pagoda southern entrance to Chinatown **(right)** was inspired by traditional Chinese village gates.

❷ **Golden Gate Fortune Cookie Company**
Fortune cookies were invented in San Francisco. Stop by to watch how the skilful workers slip the fortune message in the cookie mixture then fold it into the traditional shapes.

❸ **Chinese Six Companies**
This building's brilliant facade is one of the most ornate in Chinatown. The Six Companies association was formed in 1882 to promote Chinese interests within the community.

❹ **Portsmouth Square**
This was San Francisco's original town square – here, on July 9, 1846, the US flag was first raised when the port was seized from Mexico. Locals now use the area for tai chi and games such as mah-jongg or cards **(below)**.

❺ **St. Mary's Square**
This square is graced by a stainless-steel and rose-granite statue of Sun Yat-sen by San Francisco sculptor Beniamino Bufano.

❻ **Chinese Historical Society of America**
This building, designed by architect Julia Morgan in 1932, is the home of a learning center and a museum containing a 15,000-piece collection of artifacts, documents, photographs, and replicas that illustrate and explain the Chinese American experience.

7 Stockton Street Chinese Markets

At these popular markets (left) selling fresh produce, the real smells, sights, and sounds of Chinatown come into sharp focus.

8 Old Chinese Telephone Exchange

This three-tiered pagoda is now the East West Bank, and is the most distinctive work of architectural chinoiserie in Chinatown. It served as the telephone exchange up until the 1950s.

9 Chinese Culture Center

The Chinese Culture Center comprises an art gallery and a small crafts shop, which features the work of Chinese and Chinese American artists.

Temples 10

There are a number of temples that incorporate Confucian, Taoist, and Buddhist elements. The Tin How Temple (right), founded in 1852, is particularly worth visiting (see p62).

THE CHINESE EXCLUSION ACT

Chinese immigrants began to arrive with the Gold Rush, to get rich quick and return home heroes. However, things turned politically sour in China at the time and many people decided to stay. There was a racist backlash against those who settled, resulting in the Chinese Exclusion Act of 1882, which suspended Chinese immigration for a decade and made Chinese immigrants ineligible for naturalization. It was not until 1943 that the act was repealed.

NEED TO KNOW

Golden Gate Fortune Cookie Company: **MAP M4**; 56 Ross Alley; (415) 781-3956

Chinese Six Companies: **MAP N4**; 843 Stockton St

Chinese Historical Society of America: **MAP N5**; 965 Clay St; (415) 391-1188; www.chsa.org

Old Chinese Telephone Exchange: **MAP M4**; 743 Washington St

Chinese Culture Center: **MAP M5**; Hilton Hotel, 750 Kearny St, 3rd floor; (415) 986-1822; www.c-c-c.org

■ Don't drive into Chinatown as it's very congested, and it can be impossible to find parking.

Take the cable car instead. All three of the cable car lines will get you to the area (see p15) or stroll from the Union Square.

■ One of the most popular Chinese restaurants in San Francisco, Yank Sing (see p93), can be found here, serving Shanghai dumplings. There are also plenty of other Asian restaurants to choose from.

TOP 10 ⭐ Golden Gate Park

This is every San Franciscan's beloved backyard. Weekends draw hundreds of people here to play or relax. Almost every sort of recreational activity is available, from hiking to fishing. There's also the very first children's playground in the US, with the magnificent Herschell-Spillman Carousel, built in 1914. Even on a rainy day, the park offers world-class activities in the form of de Young Museum, the California Academy of Sciences, and Morrison Planetarium.

1 **National AIDS Memorial Grove**
This memorial, in a quiet forest hideaway, was built in remembrance of those who have died from AIDS.

2 **Stow Lake and Strawberry Hill**
Strawberry Hill is the island in the middle of this lake. Don't miss the Chinese moon-viewing pavilion on the island's eastern shore.

3 **Conservatory of Flowers**
The park's oldest building, a copy of one in London's Kew Gardens, is a Victorian Structure sheltering over 20,000 rare plants.

4 **Japanese Tea Garden**
This delightful garden is full of bonsai trees, rock gardens, native Japanese plantings, and pagodas (right).

5 **Bison Paddock**
In 1984 a small herd of bison was given a home roaming under the eucalyptus trees.

6 **Strybing Arboretum and Botanical Garden**
More than 7,000 species live in areas including a Redwood Grove, an Ancient Plant Garden, and a Garden of Fragrance.

7 **Giant Tree Fern Grove and John McLaren Rhododendron Dell**
Coming upon the Giant Tree Fern Grove, with its huge, curling proto-flora gathered around a small lagoon, is like entering a primeval forest. The Rhododendron Dell contains the largest variety (850) of these blooms in any US garden.

8 **Dutch Windmill and Queen Wilhelmina Tulip Garden**
In the northwest corner of the park, the gigantic windmill towers over the stunning tulip garden that surrounds it (left). Both were gifts from the queen of the Netherlands in 1902.

NEED TO KNOW

MAP D4 ■ Entrances on Fulton St, Lincoln Way, Stanyan St & the Great Hwy ■ (415) 831-2700 ■ www.sfrecpark.org

Open sunrise–sunset daily

Japanese Tea Garden: Hagiwara Tea Garden Drive; open Mar–Oct:

9am–5:45pm daily (Nov–Feb: to 4:45pm); adm $10-13 adults, $7 youths/seniors, $3 children; www.japanesetea gardensf.com

Strybing Arboretum and Botanical Garden: 9th Ave; opening hours vary, check website; adm $2–$8; www.sfbg.org

■ For information on the Golden Gate Park, stop at the McLaren Lodge Visitor Center *(501 Stanyan St; open 8am–5pm Mon–Fri)*.

■ At the West end of the park is the historic Beach Chalet *(see p123)*, serving lunch and dinner during the week and open for brunch on weekends.

10 Shakespeare Garden

This charming English garden **(above)** features the 200-odd flowers and herbs mentioned in the Bard's works. Bronze plaques quote the relevant passages.

Music Concourse 9

This area **(right)** hosts free events and summer concerts of a variety of genres.

A MIRACLE OF LAND RECLAMATION

The park's more than 1.5 sq miles (4 sq km) are some 3 miles (5 km) long and half a mile (1 km) wide, making it the largest cultivated urban park in the US. There are 27 miles (43 km) of footpaths, winding through lakes, gardens, waterfalls, and forests, but it was not always so. Before the 1870s, the entire area was untouched scrubland and sandbanks. William Hammond Hall made great progress over two decades, then hired Scottish gardener John McLaren in 1890. "Uncle John," as he was known, made the park his life's work, devoting himself to its perfection until his death in 1943, aged 97.

TOP 10 ⭐ California Academy of Sciences

Located in Golden Gate Park since 1916, the California Academy of Sciences now occupies a modern building. It houses the Steinhart Aquarium, Morrison Planetarium, and the Kimball Natural History Museum, and combines innovative architecture with flexible exhibition spaces. Filled with native plant species, the 2.5-acre (1-ha) living roof has been designed to help the museum blend in with the surrounding parkland.

NEED TO KNOW

MAP D4 ■ Music Concourse ■ www.calacademy.org

Open 9:30am–5pm Mon–Sat, 11am–5pm Sun

Adm fee varies, check website to book in advance

■ Take the Muni lines 5, 44, and the N-Judah to reach the museum. Save $3 on admission with proof of the use of public transportation.

■ Over 21s can explore the museum from 6–10pm on Thursdays. There is a different theme every week.

■ Admission is free four times a year (check website for details).

1 Living Roof

The museum is topped with a 108,900-sq-ft (10,100-sq-m) living roof **(above)**, which is planted with over 1.7 million native Californian plants. Take an elevator up to the rooftop deck to enjoy the views and learn about the benefits of sustainable architecture.

2 California Coast

Explore a variety of habitats ranging from salt marshes to turbulent rocky inlets and meet a variety of native fish and invertebrates. The main tank – an exhibit featuring the marine habitats of the Gulf of the Farallones National Marine Sanctuary – is 100,000 gallons in capacity, with large viewing windows, and a crashing wave surge system.

3 Discovery Tidepool

Stroke a starfish or pick up a sea slug in this hands-on attraction, which is part of the California Coast exhibits. You don't have to worry about slippery rocks to get close to these coastal creatures. The pool is staffed by volunteers who inform you about the animals and keep them safe.

4 Morrison Planetarium

Fly through space and time to the very limits of the known universe, and gain a new perspective on the planet we call home, with high-tech exhibits and technology, including an all-digital dome **(below)**. Shows are presented daily.

REDESIGN OF THE DECADE

Architect Renzo Piano redesigned the California Academy of Sciences in 2008 using sustainable materials, minimizing its energy use. At the time, this environmental marvel was the world's first to be certified Double Platinum by the U.S. Green Building Council.

8 Water Planet
Dozens of tanks and a range of interactive media are used to inform all ages of what it takes to survive under water. A variety of fish, including jellyfish, paddlefish, reptiles, amphibians, and insects are on display.

9 Philippine Coral Reef
This is one of the deepest living coral reef displays in the world. It exhibits a range of aquatic life from the reefs and mangroves of the Philippines. Sharks, rays, coral, reef fish, and colorful clams can all be seen here.

5 Osher Rainforest
Explore four rainforest habitats in a large glass dome: the Amazonian Flooded Forest, Borneo Forest Floor, Madagascar Rainforest Understory, and the Costa Rica Rainforest Canopy. The path (above) winds up in a habitat of 1,600 tropical plants and creatures, such as piranhas, flying lizards, birds, and an Amazonian boa.

7 African Hall
Magnificent dioramas display a range of taxidermied African fauna in their natural surroundings, such as the straight-horned oryx, gorillas, antelope, and cheetahs. The human evolution exhibit tracks the fascinating history of our species with fossils of our early ancestors. A lively colony of African penguins, which can be viewed through a vast window, ends the exhibit.

10 The Swamp
Part of the Steinhart Aquarium, which holds about 38,000 animals, the Swamp is home to alligator snapping turtles, Claude – the famous alligator with albinism – and frog, rattlesnake, and salamander exhibits.

6 Penguin Feeding Time
Enjoy watching the black-footed penguins waddle on land (right), or dive and glide effortlessly through the water to catch their meal, in the African Hall.

TOP 10 ⭐ de Young Museum

The immense copper-clad de Young Museum looms as a cultural and architectural landmark above a canopy of plane trees in the Music Concourse of the Golden Gate Park. It is a bastion of American, Oceanian, and African art and is home to a world-famous textile collection. The de Young also lures crowds to blockbuster temporary exhibits such as Kehinde Wiley: An Archaeology of Silence, and the popular Obama Portraits Tour.

1 Textiles and Costumes

Three centuries of fiber art and fashion include bark cloth, Central Asian and North Indian silks, the most important Anatolian kilims outside Turkey **(above)**, European tapestries, and early 20th-century couture.

2 Hamon Observation Tower

It's free to ascend the 144-ft (43.8-m) tower to the 360-degree glass-walled observation deck **(below)** for treetop views of the Music Concourse, the park, the city, and beyond to the Golden Gate Bridge and the Marin Headlands.

3 Photography

Spanning the history of the medium, the de Young is strong on 19th-century American and European images, from documentation of the 1894 California Midwinter International Exposition and daguerreotypes to early and contemporary San Franciscan scenes.

4 Temporary Exhibits

Wildly popular and requiring advance tickets, some blockbuster exhibitions have included Tutankhamun's treasures and retrospectives on artists Ed Ruscha and Frank Stella.

5 20th-Century American and Bay Area Artists

Georgia O'Keeffe's *Petunias* is among the contemporary masterworks on display, along with those of local icons – Chiura Obata, Wayne Thiebaud, and Ruth Asawa. It also features a major acquisition of works by African Americans.

The museum gardens

6 Museum Gardens

Explore the remnants of the California Midwinter International Exposition of 1894 in the surrounding shady walking trails: the Pool of Enchantment, the vases, and the sphinxes **(left)**.

7 Artful Kids

The de Young welcomes kids to free Saturday art classes, summer camps, and a monthly artist-in-residence workshop for the whole family. Guided tours for families are followed by studio workshops taught by professional artists.

⑩ American Collection

Founded by donations from the Rockefellers, this comprehensive collection, from 1670 to the present, has more than 3,000 decorative arts objects, 800 sculptures, and 1,000 paintings, including *Boatmen on the Missouri* **(left)** by George Caleb Bingham.

MORE AT THE DE YOUNG MUSEUM

Take breaks from total art immersion at the de Young by enjoying the indoor-outdoor café and the rambling sculpture garden (you can come in and out of the museum all day with your ticket). Audio and docent-led tours enrich the experience, as do curator talks and workshops. Art enthusiasts flock to the "Friday Nights at the de Young" events of music, panels, and interaction with artists, during which cocktails are served. The two-level store is stocked with art books, exhibit programs, logo items, and signature jewelry, textiles, posters, and prints relating to the exhibits. Kids can spend some time in the toy- and book-filled children's section.

⑧ Art of the Americas

Pre-Columbian and ancient Native American artifacts are displayed in these galleries, including a stunning group of Teotihuacan murals. The Weisel Family Collection spans 1,000 years of Native American objects and textiles.

⑨ Africa and the Pacific

Micronesian and Maori carvings, basketry, and over 1,400 pieces from across the regions are on view, along with Scheller's collection of Masterworks of African Figurative Sculpture **(below)**, depicting 140 ethnic groups.

NEED TO KNOW

MAP C4 ■ 50 Hagiwara Tea Garden Drive, Golden Gate Park ■ (415) 750-3600 ■ www.deyoung.famsf.org

Open 9:30am–5:15pm Tue–Sun (to 8:30pm on selected Fri; check website for details)

Adm $15 adult, $12 senior, $6 student/youth, under 18s free; free on first Tue of month; limited-run exhibitions may require separate tickets purchased in advance

■ The de Young is accessible via bus – the 44 O'Shaughnessy and the 5 and 5R Fulton. Save $2 on admission with proof of public transit. Self-parking is available under the museum.

■ Children are welcome, although large bags are forbidden and strollers are not allowed in some venues.

■ Same-day free admission to the Legion of Honor museum *(see p117)* with a de Young ticket.

Following pages Rolling vineyards in Sonoma County

TOP 10 ⭐ San Francisco Museum of Modern Art

Standing proudly next to Yerba Buena Gardens art complex, SFMOMA forms the nucleus of San Francisco's reputation as a leading center of modern art. Created in 1935, it moved into its current quarters in 1995, and in May 2016 reopened after a major three-year $305 million expansion that tripled its gallery space. The museum offers a dynamic schedule of special exhibitions and permanent collection presentations.

1 Outdoor Terraces
Six outdoor terraces provide spaces for sculpture installations and highlight dramatic cityscape views.

2 Photography
A highlight of the museum; the 15,000 sq ft (1, 394 sq m) Pritzker Center for Photography houses a collection of over 17,800 photographs.

3 Exterior
The facade of the Snøhetta expansion **(below)** comprises more than 700 uniquely-shaped panels which appear to shift in appearance with the changing light.

4 20th-Century American Artists
US artists included here are O'Keeffe, de Kooning, Pollock, Warhol, and Kline. One of the perennial hits is an iconic ceramic sculpture named *Michael Jackson and Bubbles* by Jeff Koons (1988).

5 Media Arts
Established in 1988, this impressive collection includes multimedia works, moving-image pieces, and video installations by such artists as Brian Eno, Dara Birnbaum, Bill Viola, and Nam June Paik.

6 The Living Wall
This incredible living wall provides a unique background for sculpture on the third floor terrace. Populated with 19,000 plants, including 21 native plant species, it is an ever-changing work of natural art.

7 Special Exhibitions
The museum's special exhibition spaces may feature retrospective exhibitions of the work of modern and contemporary artists, such as multimedia artist Yoko Ono, sculptor Eva Hesse, and artist Robert Rauschenberg.

Key
- First floor
- Second floor
- Third floor
- Fourth floor
- Fifth floor
- Sixth floor
- Seventh floor

San Francisco Museum of Modern Art

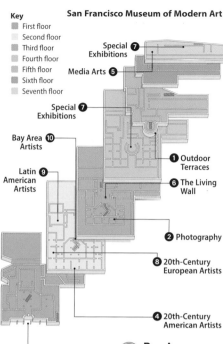

Special Exhibitions **7**

Media Arts **5**

Special Exhibitions **7**

Bay Area Artists **10**

Latin American Artists **9**

1 Outdoor Terraces

6 The Living Wall

2 Photography

8 20th-Century European Artists

4 20th-Century American Artists

3 Exterior

NEED TO KNOW

MAP Q5 ■ 151 3rd St ■ (415) 357-4000 ■ www.sfmoma.org

Open 10am–5pm Fri–Tue (to 8pm Thu)

Adm $25 adult, $22 senior (65 years and older), $19 19–24 years with ID, under-18s free; audio tour price varies

Museum store: open 11am–5pm Fri–Tue & 1–8pm Thu; closed Wed

■ Across 3rd Street from SFMOMA, Yerba Buena Gardens *(see pp34–5)* offers more galleries, museums, and attractions.

■ The family-friendly Cafe 5 is in the sculpture garden at SFMOMA. For fine dining, head to In Situ, on the first floor. Sightglass, on the third floor, serves coffee and pastries.

■ The museum store has various art books, stationery, and fashion accessories.

Museum Guide

The ground floor welcomes visitors with free art-filled public spaces and galleries. Works from the permanent collection are on the second floor, as are galleries for works on paper and Californian art. The Pritzker Center for Photography is located on the third floor, whilst the Doris and Donald Fisher Collection begins on the third floor and continues in the Fisher Galleries on the fourth, fifth, and sixth floors. The seventh floor showcases contemporary works and media arts.

8 20th-Century European Artists

Works by 20th-century European artists are located on the second floor. Here you will find important works by Matisse, Miró, Klee, Picasso, Braque, Mondrian, Duchamp, Dalí, and Magritte, among others.

Latin American Artists **9**

Latin American art is represented here by the work of muralist Diego Rivera and Frida Kahlo. Other Latin American representation includes architect Tatiana Bilbao's model *(Not) Another Tower* **(right)**.

10 Bay Area Artists

San Francisco Bay Area artists with international reputations on display include Clyfford Still, Richard Diebenkorn, and Wayne Thiebaud. Bay Area figurative painters in the collection include Elmer Bischoff and David Park. Most noteworthy, perhaps, is *California Artist* (1982), a sculptural self-portrait by Robert Arneson in glazed stoneware.

Yerba Buena Gardens

Skyscrapers around Yerba Buena Gardens

1 Yerba Buena Center for the Arts Gallery

MAP Q5 ▪ 701 Mission St ▪ (415) 978-2700 ▪ Open noon–6pm Thu–Sun ▪ Adm ▪ www.ybca.org

Changing exhibitions here explore issues of race, class, gender, history, technology, and art.

2 Yerba Buena Center for the Arts Theater

MAP Q5 ▪ Box Office: (415) 978-2787

Diversity is at the heart of this 750-seat indoor theater, so the range of performances can include world-music festivals or Victorian operettas.

3 Moscone Center

MAP Q5 ▪ Howard St

This building began the renovation of the SoMa district. Most of it is underground; above ground the impression is of glass, girders, and gardens.

4 Metreon

MAP Q4 ▪ 101 4th St

The main attraction at this shopping center is a state-of-the-art movie theater (including IMAX screens). On the fourth floor is a pleasant terrace with superb views of the cityscape.

5 Rooftop Children's Center and Carousel

MAP Q5 ▪ 750 Folsom St

The carousel in this complex dates from 1906. There's also an ice-skating rink, a bowling alley, a learning garden, and an amphitheater.

6 Children's Creativity Museum

MAP Q5 ▪ 221 4th St ▪ (415) 820-3320 ▪ Opening hours vary, check website ▪ Adm ▪ www.creativity.org

This interactive technology and art museum aims to inspire children's creative impulses. There are animation, design, and music studios.

7 California Historical Society

MAP P5 ▪ 678 Mission St ▪ (415) 357-1848 ▪ Open noon–5:30pm Thu & Fri ▪ Adm

This research organization holds vast collections of photos, books, maps, manuscripts, prints, and arts, some dating as far back as the 1600s.

8 Martin Luther King, Jr. Memorial

Featuring words of peace in several languages, this multifaceted monument incorporates sculpture, a waterfall, and quotations from the speeches and writings of the Civil Rights leader.

⑨ Contemporary Jewish Museum (CJM)

MAP P5 ▪ 736 Mission St between 3rd and 4th ▪ (415) 655-7800 ▪ Open 11am–5pm Thu–Sun ▪ Closed Mon–Wed, Jewish hols, & some public hols ▪ Adm ▪ www.thecjm.org

This dynamic museum *(see p51)* was designed by architect Daniel Libeskind and incorporates the landmark Jesse Street Power Substation. The museum's exhibits present a variety of art, photography, and installations celebrating and exploring Judaism.

Contemporary Jewish Museum

⑩ Esplanade
www.ybgfestival.org

The Esplanade comprises garden-lined walkways, an inviting lawn, rolling hills, trees, and interesting sculptures. There is a free weekly concert here during the summer festival.

THE RISE OF SOUTH OF MARKET

Formerly an unattractive and dangerous industrial area of warehouses and factories, the SoMa district began its transformation in the 1970s, when the area was redeveloped following the construction of the Moscone Center. Upscale interior designer showrooms emerged, along with trendy nightclubs and restaurants, high-rise hotels and office buildings, as well as museums and galleries. The three buildings of the Moscone Center comprise more than 1,000,000-sq-ft (93,000-sq-m) of exhibition and meeting spaces. The whole district is now seen as a desirable neighborhood.

TOP 10 NOTABLE CONSTRUCTIONS SOUTH OF MARKET

1 Oracle Park
2 SFMOMA
3 Moscone Center
4 Yerba Buena Center
5 Rincon Center
6 Salesforce Transit Center
7 South Park
8 Salesforce Tower
9 Millennium Tower
10 The Four Seasons and the Marriott hotels

The Moscone Center has a 200,000-sq-ft (186,000-sq-m) glass-enclosed expansion at 3rd and Howard Streets, which cost $551 million to build. It is an architectural highlight of the South of Market district.

🔟 ⭐ Wine Country

The world-famous Wine Country comprises two picturesque valleys, Napa and Sonoma, the hills and dales surrounding them, and over 400 wineries. Napa is more developed for visitors, while Sonoma is more low-key but equally inviting. Napa's downtown area has also become a popular destination for fine dining, tasting rooms, and boutique accommodations.

① Napa Valley Wine Train

Leaving from Napa and arriving in St. Helena, or vice versa, you can avoid the traffic and partake of a gourmet meal complemented by local wines. The trip takes 3 hours in total and the train (below) features a 1915 Pullman dining car.

② Sterling Vineyards

A tram provides a unique way to experience both the landscape and wine.

③ Beringer Vineyards

The oldest Napa Valley winery (below), established in 1876. Tours, including a self-guided tour, consist of a visit to the 1,000-ft (300-m) wine tunnels, which were carved by hand out of volcanic stone.

④ Clos Pegase

Housed in an award-winning Post-Modern structure, this beguiling winery offers tours and tastings and features an extensive collection of modern art. The wine is memorable, too – specialties include Cabernet, Merlot, and Portico port.

⑤ Yountville

Hot-air balloons float in the sky over the village of Yountville, where sweet cottages share the tree-lined streets with restaurants, galleries, upscale hotels, and V Marketplace, a gigantic brick edifice that houses shops, cafés, a spa, and wine-tasting salons.

Wine Country

⑥ The Culinary Institute of America

An impressive castle-like landmark, built in about 1890, houses the West Coast annex of the Culinary Institute of America. Foodies can stock up at the gourmet store, peruse the museum, or enjoy cookery and wine classes. The restaurant, with a terrace overlooking the vineyard, serves regional cuisine paired with appropriate wines.

7 Sonoma

This appealing town, nestled in the Valley of the Moon **(below)**, is filled with high-end restaurants, small hotels, and shops. The town also features a State Historic Park with a mission building and structures dating from the early to mid-1800s.

CALIFORNIA WINE

Since 1857, wine-making has been the mainstay of this area. A phylloxera blight in the early 1900s nearly put an end to it all, but Europe was hit harder, and it was the resistant California vines that brought back the wine business to parts of Italy, France, and Spain. In 1976 California wines were put on the international map, when they trounced France in a blind taste-test in Paris. These days, many European producers also have wineries in California.

10 Hess Collection

The tours here are a pleasure, including not only wine-making facilities but also the owner's gallery of contemporary European and American artists. The Cabernet Sauvignon, Merlot, and Chardonnay **(right)** are all very good.

8 Domaine Chandon

Lovely gardens, a fine restaurant, and sweeping views complement the sparkling, champagne-style wines of this Moët Hennessy showcase, which produces 500,000 cases every year.

9 Castello di Amorosa

This recreation of a Tuscan Medieval castle has a moat, watchtowers and a draw-bridge as well as a torture chamber. Take a guided tour and taste the Italian-style wines produced here.

NEED TO KNOW

Napa Valley Wine Train: 1275 McKinstry St, Napa; (707) 253-2111; www. winetrain.com

Sterling Vineyards: 1111 Dunaweal Lane, Calistoga; (800) 726-6136; www.sterlingvineyards.com

Beringer Vineyards: 2000 Main St, St. Helena; (707) 257-5771; www. beringer.com

Clos Pegase: 1060 Dunaweal Lane, Calistoga; (707) 942-4981; www.clos pegase.com

The Culinary Institute of America: 2555 Main St, St. Helena; (707) 967-1100; www.cia chef.edu

Domaine Chandon: 1 California Drive, Yountville; (888) 242-6366; www.chandon.com

Castello di Amorosa: 4045 St. Helena Hwy, Calistoga; (707) 967-6272; www.castellodi amorosa.com

Hess Collection: 4411 Redwood Rd, Napa; (707) 255-1144; www. hessperssonestates.com

■ For very special snacks, try the Model Bakery at 1357 Main St in St. Helena.

Wine Country Spas

1 Fairmont Sonoma Mission Inn & Spa
100 Boyes Blvd, Sonoma ■ **(707) 938-9000** ■ **www.fairmont.com/sonoma**

This famous inn provides an oasis of ultimate indulgence in luxury and refinement. Blessed by natural mineral hot springs, the legendary spa, with inspired architecture and lovely landscaping, exudes understated opulence and serenity.

Fairmont Sonoma Mission Inn & Spa

2 Indian Springs Calistoga
1712 Lincoln Ave, Calistoga ■ **(707) 942-4913** ■ **www.indianspringscalistoga.com**

Dating from 1862, this hot springs resort with mineral waters from natural geysers has been modernized but has an old-fashioned air about it, with an Olympic-sized heated pool, extensive gardens, and professional spa and mud bath treatments. On-site are lodge rooms and pretty cottages with fireplaces, kitchens, and air-conditioning. There's also a casual restaurant and bar.

3 Health Spa Napa Valley
1030 Main St, St. Helena ■ **(707) 967-8800** ■ **www.napavalleyspa.com**

In a serene, open-air setting, aches and anxieties are alleviated with a plethora of pampering rituals. For some, that may mean a stimulating fitness workout, or a soothing mud wrap and massage overlooking the tranquil Spa Garden.

4 The Kenwood Inn and Spa
10400 Sonoma Hwy, Kenwood ■ **(707) 833-1293** ■ **www.kenwoodinn.com**

Nationally acclaimed as one of the Wine Country's most elegant and intimate country inns, the Kenwood consists of lovely guest suites and a full-service spa facility. The inn has the ambience of an Italian country villa in the Sonoma Valley, situated on a secluded hillside facing over 1.5 sq miles (4 sq km) of vineyards. The spa offers a variety of massage styles, including aromatherapy and Ayurvedic.

5 Calistoga Spa Hot Springs
1006 Washington St, Calistoga ■ **(707) 942-6269** ■ **www.calistogaspa.com**

Just off the main street, soak in the four outdoor geothermal mineral pools (with a wading pool for kids). Try a mud bath, use the gym, or take a yoga or Pilates class. Accommodations include contemporary rooms with kitchenettes.

6 Mount View Hotel & Spa
1457 Lincoln Ave, Calistoga ■ **(707) 942-6877** ■ **www.mountviewhotel.com**

A stay in this historic 1917 resort offers various relaxation and rejuvenation possibilities – mud, milk, or herbal baths, aromatherapy steam showers, body wraps, massages, or facials – geared to individuals or couples.

7 Meritage Resort and Spa
875 Bordeaux Way, Napa ■ (844) 283-4588 ■ www.meritageresort.com

Silence and serenity abide in this luxury resort. The stone-walled, Old World-style "Estate Cave" contains 12 treatment rooms, with whirlpools and saunas. The four-star hotel rooms are spacious; ask about the special packages on offer. On site, you will find restaurants, a large fitness studio, and a sports bar.

Meritage Resort and Spa

8 Silverado Resort and Spa
1600 Atlas Peak Rd, Napa ■ (707) 257-0200 ■ www.silveradoresort.com

On 2 sq miles (5 sq km), studded by oak trees and anchored by a historic mansion housing restaurants and lounges, this luxury resort in the Wine Country has two championship golf courses, dozens of swimming pools, and a tennis complex. The upscale spa offers 12 rooms for top-notch body treatments, plus private garden pavilions, a nail and hair salon, a café, yoga classes, and workout facilities.

9 Villagio Inn and Spa
6481 Washington St, Yountville ■ (707) 944-8877 ■ www.villagio.com

Fireplaces, water features, and lush gardens create rustic luxury, to be enjoyed in the 16 treatment rooms with Swiss showers, saunas, and secluded outdoor baths. Spa suites for couples are romantic enclosures with soaking tubs, fireplaces, steam showers, and private terraces. At the associated four-star Villagio Inn, spacious rooms are surrounded by gardens adorned with replicas of Greek and Roman statuary.

10 Boon Hotel + Spa
14711 Armstrong Woods Rd, Guerneville ■ (707) 869-2721 ■ www.boonhotels.com

In the beautiful redwoods of the Russian River area, this small, peaceful, adults-only inn offers an invigorating retreat from modern life. Body treatments include deep-tissue and hot-stone massages, and soothing facials with seaweed anti-wrinkle masks. Included in your stay are use of the pool and Jacuzzi, and evening wine-tastings on selected weekends. The restaurant serves Russian River wines, and sources ingredients from local suppliers or from its garden.

Championship golf course at Silverado Resort and Spa

The Top 10 of Everything

Interior of Grace Cathedral

🔟 Moments in History

A depiction of San Francisco in the mid-19th century

1 Native Americans

There were settlements in the Bay as early as the 11th century BCE, made up of hunters and gatherers who enjoyed a rich diet of seeds, shellfish, and game. We know now these people made up three distinct Indigenous groups: Coast Miwok, the Wintun, and the Ohlone.

2 European Arrival

In 1579, English explorer Sir Frances Drake landed near Point Reyes and claimed Alta California for Queen Elizabeth I, marking the beginning of European colonization in the Bay Area. However, Drake and many other early explorers failed to travel beyond the straits, which were later used by the Spanish to establish dominance in the region.

3 Spanish Conquest

By the late 1700s, the Spanish began establishing a presence in and around San Francisco. In 1776, an expedition led by Juan Bautista de Anza arrived at San Francisco Bay. Their arrival had a devastating effect on local Indigenous populations, exposing them to foreign diseases and forcing the communities into enslavement.

4 American Takeover

Impending war with Mexico in the 1840s inspired US leaders to arouse the interest of Bay Area settlers in joining the Union. In 1846, a party of Yankees in Sonoma declared California's independence from Mexico. Shortly after, Commodore John Sloat claimed California as US territory.

5 Gold Rush Days

In 1848 the carpenter James Wilson Marshall noticed a glitter in the sediment of the American River in the Sierra Nevada foothills while building a mill for John Sutter, and realized it was gold. Word leaked out, and businessman Sam Brannan displayed a bottle of gold dust and

News of gold reaches New York

nuggets. The subsequent stampede of prospectors, dubbed the '49ers, made the city a boomtown overnight.

6 First Mayor of San Francisco

Francisco de Haro was the *alcalde* (mayor) of the pueblo of Yerba Buena under Mexican rule. When the Mexican War in California ended in favor of the US, the city became San Francisco. John W. Geary, elected at age 31, became its first mayor.

7 Panama-Pacific Exposition

Held in 1915 to celebrate the opening of the Panama Canal, the real *raison d'être* for the festivities was that San Franciscans had resurrected their city after the 1906 earthquake that destroyed 80 per cent of the city.

8 Bay and Golden Gate Bridges

The inauguration of the Bay Bridge in 1936 heralded the end of the age of ferryboats by linking the city to the East Bay. The inauguration of the Golden Gate Bridge *(see pp12–13)* took place a year later.

9 Summer of Love

San Francisco counterculture burst forth in the summer of 1967. Hippies were everywhere, and the poetry and music that embodied a new way of thinking filled the air. It was a sociopolitical shift that went on to influence the whole world.

10 Modern Parity

In 1992, California was the first state to send two female Senators, Dianne Feinstein and Barbara Boxer, to the US Congress. As of 2019, boards of corporations based in the state are required to have at least one woman at the table.

Dianne Feinstein

TOP 10 SCANDALS AND DISASTERS

Allen Ginsberg
(1926–1997)
Renowned poet, leading figure of the Beat Generation of American writers and artists, champion of freedom of expression and sexual self-determination

The author of *Howl*, Allen Ginsberg

1 Genocide of Native Americans
By the late 1800s, the spread of Eurasian diseases and bounties placed on the capture of Indigenous peoples decimated Native American communities.

2 Gold Rush Lawlessness
Gold Rush frontier life was so criminal that vigilante justice was proclaimed in the 1850s, leading to secret trials.

3 1906
An earthquake and consequent fire devastated much of the city, and 250,000 people were left homeless.

4 "Bloody Thursday"
On July 5, 1934, the police fired shots at longshoremen who were on strike, leaving two of them dead.

5 Howl
On October 13, 1955, Allen Ginsberg read out this revolutionary poem, which was later banned as obscene, at the Six Gallery in San Francisco.

6 Freedom and Anti-War Riots
Pro-Civil Rights and anti-Vietnam War riots occurred from 1964 to 1970.

7 Death of a Rock Icon
Part of hippie legend, Janis Joplin died of a heroin overdose in 1970.

8 White's Revenge
In 1978 ex-Supervisor Dan White shot dead Mayor George Moscone and gay Supervisor Harvey Milk *(see p45)*. He was controversially convicted of manslaughter rather than murder.

9 AIDS
The epidemic reached overwhelming proportions in the city in the 1980s, taking the lives of many.

10 Loma Prieta Earthquake
In October 1989, the quake destroyed the Victorian center of Santa Cruz *(see p83)* and part of the Bay Bridge.

🔟 Historic Sites

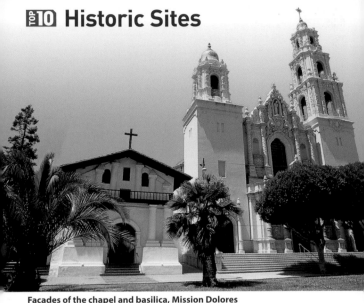

Facades of the chapel and basilica, Mission Dolores

1 Mission Dolores

This 18th-century Spanish mission *(see p109)* is the oldest building in the city. Its 4 ft (1.2 m) thick adobe walls and red-tile roofs are typical of the "Mission Style" seen all over California.

2 Jackson Square

This area *(see p88)* contains some of the city's oldest, loveliest buildings. One of the few places spared in the 1906 conflagration.

3 Nob Hill

Home to historic hotels and remnants of the age of prosperity of the railroad barons *(see p87)*. The Fairmont Hotel (1907) is famous for the Tonga Room & Hurricane Bar, and the Mark Hopkins (1939) is crowned by the Top of the Mark lounge. Grace Cathedral's spires tower over all.

4 The Presidio

More than 350 buildings, which spent 200 years in a military enclave, have been repurposed as museums, restaurants, and recreational facilities *(see pp98–9)*. Highlights are a National Cemetery, Civil War barracks, Victorian mansions, a World War II memorial, the Walt Disney Family Museum, the Society of California Pioneers Museum, and the heritage gallery in the Officers' Club.

5 War Memorial Opera House

Inaugurated in 1932, this building *(see p66)* is dedicated to World War I soldiers. In 1945 it hosted the plenary sessions that preceded the founding of the UN and, in 1951, it was the site of the signing of the peace treaty between the US and Japan.

Huntington Park Fountain, Nob Hill

6 North Beach

This entire area *(see p87)* resonates with the history of the early Italian residents, but even more with the iconoclastic legacy of the Beats, who brought the neighborhood worldwide fame. Historic churches and the City Lights Bookstore *(see p90)* stand as clear landmarks, while equally historic saloons and cafés are worth seeking out.

7 Haight-Ashbury

The matrix of yet another alternative movement that San Francisco has given birth to, this area *(see p104)* nurtured idealistic hippies in the late 1960s. They brought international awareness to alternative ways of life, living in harmony with nature.

8 The Fillmore

MAP E3 ■ **1805 Geary Blvd**

One of the legendary homes *(see pp66–7)* of psychedelic rock during the 1960s. Along with the Avalon Ballroom and the Winterland (both now gone), this is where the San Francisco sound found its first audience.

9 Ferry Building Marketplace

MAP H2 ■ **Embarcadero at Market**

Once the tallest building in the city *(see p76)*, with a 235-ft- (71.6-m-) high clock tower modeled after the Giralda tower in Seville, in 1898 this was the headquarters of streetcars and ferryboats. Fireboat crews saved the tower from the 1906 fire.

10 Fort Point National Historic Site

MAP C1 ■ **Marine Drive**

At this much-photographed site *(see p78)* under the Golden Gate Bridge, swords, guns, and cannons are on view at a fortification that was built during the Civil War to pro- tect the city from an attack by sea, which never came. Rangers and costumed docents give free tours of the gunpowder storehouse, the barracks, and the museum.

TOP 10 HISTORIC FIGURES

Photograph of John Muir

1 John Muir
A keen promoter of the National Parks movement. The Muir Woods *(see p82)* are named in his honor.

2 John C. Fremont
Instrumental in the US annexation of California in the mid-1800s, Fremont dubbed the Bay strait the "Golden Gate."

3 Ansel Adams
Born in 1902, Adams was a well-known photographer and environmentalist. His work later became important for local conservation.

4 Leland Stanford
One of the "Big Four" who masterminded the Transcontinental Railroad, he also founded Stanford University *(see p126)*.

5 Dr. Dian Fossey
One of the world's foremost experts on primatology, Dr. Fossey helped pave the way for women in zoological studies.

6 Isadora Duncan
This pioneer of modern dance lived a life of creativity and adventure.

7 Dorothea Lange
An acclaimed photojournalist known for documenting the plight of common folks during the 1930s Great Depression.

8 Harvey Milk
The first openly gay politician to become a member of the Board of Supervisors was assassinated in 1978.

9 Dianne Feinstein
One of the movers and shakers of San Francisco politics in recent decades, she became a US Senator in 1992.

10 Jerry Brown
The four-term Governor of California, and the longest-serving governor in state history. He was once Mayor of Oakland and also ran for US President.

🔟 Religious Centers

Cathedral of St. Mary of the Assumption

1 Cathedral of St. Mary of the Assumption

MAP F3 ▪ 1111 Gough St ▪ (415) 567-2020 ▪ Services: 7:30am & 12:20pm Mon–Fri; 8am & 5:30pm Sat; 7:30am, 9am, 11am & 1pm (Spanish) Sun ▪ www.stmarycathedralsf.org

The cast concrete walls of this 1971 brutalist structure meet in a cross of stained glass some 18 storeys above a vast interior, creating a uniquely contemplative modernist space.

2 Grace Cathedral

The Notre Dame of San Francisco (see p87) mixes Italian Renaissance with Gothic architecture and a lot of American originality.

3 Temple Emanu-El

MAP D3 ▪ 2 Lake Street ▪ www.emanuelsf.org

This beautiful 1926 synagogue with its soaring dome was inspired by Hagia Sophia in Istanbul. Its congregation, the city's oldest, is active in philanthropy and social justice.

4 Mission Dolores

Photos and a diorama offer a stirring impression of what life was like for the Indigenous Ohlone people, who built this Spanish mission (see p109) in the 18th century.

5 Zen Center

MAP F4 ▪ 300 Page St ▪ Office hours: 9:30am–12:30pm & 1:30–4pm Mon–Fri ▪ www.sfzc.org

In addition to offering daily meditation, regular monastic retreats, workshops, lectures, and classes, the San Francisco Zen Center engages in community outreach programs as well as working for peace and protection of the environment.

6 Glide Memorial United Methodist Church

MAP Q3 ▪ 330 Ellis St ▪ (415) 674-6000 ▪ Services: 9am & 11am Sun ▪ www.glide.org

Glide Church seeks to make an impact through works that transform lives and build an inclusive, empowered community. Exuberant Sunday celebrations of community and faith are a wonderful experience.

7 Saints Peter and Paul Church

North Beach's "Italian Cathedral" was once called the "Marzipan Church" (see p90) for the stucco decoration on its soaring pinnacles. Inside, there is a sculpted reproduction of Leonardo da Vinci's *Last Supper*.

Stained glass, Saints Peter and Paul Church

(8) Tin How Temple
MAP G2 ■ 125 Waverly Pl
■ (415) 986-2520

The beautiful Tin How Temple, a spiritual center of Chinatown since the 1850s, honors the Taoist goddess of the sea, also known as Mazu. The goddess is particularly significant to those who braved the sea's perils to reach San Francisco and to their descendants.

Art by Mark Dukes, St. John Coltrane African Orthodox Church

(9) St. John Coltrane African Orthodox Church
MAP E3 ■ St. Cyprian's Episcopal Church, 2097 Turk St ■ (415) 673-7144 ■ Services: noon Sun ■ www.coltranechurch.org

"My music is the spiritual expression of what I am" said the jazz musician St. John Coltrane who is canonized by this welcoming congregation. Services consist of a sermon and worship music. Every first Sunday, service starts with the songs from his classic album *A Love Supreme*.

(10) First Unitarian Universalist Church
MAP P1 ■ 1187 Franklin St ■ (415) 776-4580 ■ Services: 11am Sun ■ www.uusf.org

Since 1850, this church has been a progressive voice in San Francisco. Welcoming all faiths and creeds, this congregation is not bound by a single faith, but by shared values.

TOP 10 CONTEMPLATIVE PLACES

Exterior of Kong Chow Temple

1 Kong Chow Temple
Chinatown's oldest temple is dedicated to Guan Di, a male deity.

2 The Japanese Garden
MAP D4 ■ 75 Hagiwara Tea Garden Drive
A peaceful space to meditate.

3 Congregation Sherith Israel
MAP F3 ■ 2266 California St ■ Services: 6pm Fri, 9:15am Sat ■ www.sherithisrael.org
Founded in 1849 by Jewish pioneers, the domed synagogue dates from 1904.

4 Vedanta Temple
MAP M5 ■ 2323 Vallejo St ■ sfvedanta.org
This was the first Hindu temple (1905) in the western world.

5 The Wave Organ
A mesmerizing wave activated sculpture at the Exploratorium (*see p88*).

6 Crystal Way
MAP F5 ■ 2335 Market St
Healing through crystals, light, sound, and positive thinking are explored.

7 Shambhala Meditation Center
MAP F4 ■ 1231 Stevenson St ■ www.shambhala.org
Meditations, talks, and classes.

8 Spirit Rock Meditation Center
5000 Sir Francis Drake Blvd, Woodacre ■ www.spiritrock.org
This center helps people find peace through meditation.

9 Kabuki Springs and Spa
MAP F3 ■ 1750 Geary Blvd
Cleanse your body and mind here.

10 Open Secret
923 C St, San Rafael ■ www.opensecretbookstore.com
The backroom of this New Age venue is like a temple to all the world's deities.

▣⑩ Architectural Highlights

① Civic Center

This complex *(see p89)* is centered on City Hall, a Baroque Revival paragon (1915) with a golden dome, attracting tourists and wedding parties for photos on its curving marble staircase decorated with filigree iron and gilt. The other buildings are in Beaux Arts style. Befitting the city that started the Gold Rush, gilt is everywhere.

Staircase of City Hall, Civic Center

② Transamerica Pyramid
MAP N5 ■ 600 Montgomery St

A sparkling white obelisk made out of crushed quartz, the pyramid is an iconic symbol of the city. At 853 ft (260 m), it is the second tallest building in San Francisco. At its base is Redwood Park, where office workers relax on weekdays. Shop for souvenirs and exhibits in the lobby.

③ 555 California Street
MAP N5 ■ 555 California St

This 52-story structure, known previously as the Bank of America Center, was the first skyscraper in the city, erected in 1972. The color was a mistake – the granite that faces it was supposed to be pink, not brown, but by the time the delivery was made, it was too late to change it.

④ San Francisco Museum of Modern Art

This striking post-modern oculus *(see pp32–3)* was designed by architect Mario Botta. It was augmented by the Norwegian firm, Snøhetta, with a rippling facade replicating the waters and fog of San Francisco Bay.

⑤ Palace of Fine Arts
MAP E1 ■ 3301 Lyon St ■ (415) 563-6504 ■ www.palaceoffinearts.org

This Neo-Classical building, today used for shows, was designed by Bernard Maybeck for the Pan-Pacific Exposition of 1915 and inspired by the engravings of Giovanni Piranesi.

⑥ Cathedral of St. Mary of the Assumption

Some critics dismiss this parabolic form *(see p46)*, but the soaring curves take attention upward, in the same way that tracery and vaulting do in Gothic cathedrals.

⑦ Coit Tower

This Art Deco landmark is named for the benefactor Lillie Coit, who left a substantial bequest to beautify her beloved

Coit Tower, Telegraph Hill

city. The observation deck offers great views. Depression-era murals *(see p90)* decorate the lobby.

French-Gothic facade, Grace Cathedral

8 Grace Cathedral

The third largest Episcopal church *(see p87)* in the US was executed in the medieval French Gothic style. Its stained-glass windows glow atop Nob Hill.

9 Haas-Lilienthal House

MAP M1 ▪ 2007 Franklin St ▪ (415) 441-3000 ▪ Tours: noon, 1pm & 2 pm Sat & Sun ▪ Adm ▪ www.haas-lilienthalhouse.org

This Queen Anne-style mansion, built in 1886, is one of the few Victorian beauties in the city that accepts visitors. It's a wonderful glimpse into the way of life among San Francisco's upper-middle classes from about 1890 to 1920. Gables, a turret, and fancy embellishments make this a showstopper on Franklin Street.

10 Alamo Square

MAP E4

With a downtown backdrop and a sweeping greensward below, these vividly hued late 1800s Victorian mansions (or "Painted Ladies") are on the 700 block of Steiner Street. The surrounding streets features gems built between the 1870s and 1920s.

TOP 10 PUBLIC ART SITES

1 Balmy Alley
MAP G6 ▪ 24th & 25th Sts between Harrison & Treat
The most famous set of murals in town, by local Latin American artists.

2 San Francisco Art Institute
MAP K3 ▪ 800 Chestnut St
Diego Rivera, the Mexican muralist, painted *The Making of a Fresco* here.

3 Bay Lights
This installation of 25,000 LED lights on the Bay Bridge is the work of Leo Villareal.

4 Fort Mason
Oliver DiCicco's *Bow Seat (see p56)* pays homage to boats on the Bay.

5 Women's Building
MAP F5 ▪ 18th St between Valencia & Guerrero
The work of seven women painters graces the facade.

6 Bikeway
MAP F4 ▪ Duboce St between Church & Market
This mural chronicles a bike ride from Downtown to Ocean Beach.

7 Golden Gate Park
The Music Concourse is home to many sculptures, including the bronze *Apple Cider Press (see pp24–5)*.

8 Rincon Center
MAP H2 ▪ Mission, Howard, Steuart & Spear Sts
These 1948 murals by Russian Anton Refregier trace Californian history.

9 Financial District
See *Transcendence* in front of 555 California Street and the Day to Night lights atop the Salesforce Tower.

10 Beach Chalet
Depression-era murals depicting famous San Franciscans *(see p123)*.

Beach Chalet mural

🔟 Museums

1 de Young Museum

This bastion *(see pp28–9)* of American, Oceanian, and African art is a landmark in Golden Gate Park, topped by a 144-ft (44-m) observation tower. Founded with pieces from the 1894 California Midwinter Fair, the Oceanic and African groupings have been expanded with private collections. There is a sculpture garden and a collection of American art from colonial times to the 20th century.

2 California Academy of Sciences

The environmentally friendly architecture of the Academy's building *(see pp26–7)* emphasizes ecological and sustainable features and blends in with the natural surroundings of the park. The museum covers virtually every aspect of the natural world.

3 Contemporary Jewish Museum (CJM)

Across the street from Yerba Buena Gardens *(see pp34–5)*, this charming 1907 Willis Polk-designed power substation was adapted by architect Daniel Libeskind in 1998. His design was inspired by the Hebrew letters that spell *chai* (life), the *chet* and the *yud*. Soaring blue steel blocks front the plaza, which change color in different light as if they were alive. The small collection of contemporary and ancient Jewish items is augmented by ever-changing exhibits covering political

Steel blocks at the plaza of CJM

art, iconic Jewish figures, immigration, architecture, modern Israel, Jewish life and culture, and more.

4 San Francisco Museum of Modern Art (SFMOMA)

The SFMOMA *(see pp32–3)* has seven levels of 20th- and 21st-century art, free public areas, outdoor terraces, a café, a restaurant, and a gift shop.

5 Asian Art Museum

MAP R2 ▪ 200 Larkin St ▪ (415) 581-3500 ▪ Open 1–8pm Thu, 10am–5pm Fri–Mon ▪ Adm ▪ www.asianart.org

Set in the old Main Library which was restructured by architect Gae Aulenti, this museum is home to a vast collection of Chinese, Korean, Japanese, Himalayan, and Southeast Asian

Korean costume, Asian Art Museum

works. On display is a collection of Chinese jade, and Buddhist art. Special exhibitions are often held here.

6 San Francisco Museum of Craft and Design

MAP H5 ■ 2569 Third St ■ (415) 773-0303 ■ Open 10am–5pm Wed–Sat, noon–5pm Sun ■ Closed major public hols ■ Adm ■ www.sfmcd.org

This unique museum celebrates modern craft and design through innovative exhibitions. Many lectures, shows, and programs are organized for children. There is also a museum store selling handmade works.

7 Museum of the African Diaspora

MAP N5 ■ 685 Mission St ■ (415) 358-4000 ■ Open 11am–6pm Wed–Sat, noon–5pm Sun ■ Adm ■ www.moadsf.org

One of the few museums dedicated to African art, the MoAD focuses on contemporary and emerging artists.

8 Society of California Pioneers

MAP D2 ■ 101 Montgomery St, Suite 150 ■ (415) 957-1849 ■ Hours vary, check website ■ www.californiapioneers.org

On display here is a collection of historical exhibits from 19th- and 20th-century California. The upstairs gallery features annually rotating exhibits from the private collection.

9 Legion of Honor

This museum (see p117) is set in a building commemorating the Californian soldiers who died in World War I. Four thousand years of ancient and European art are displayed here, as well as antiquities from ancient Egypt, Greece, and Rome.

10 Maritime Museum

MAP F1 ■ 900 Beach St, Aquatic Park ■ (415) 447-5000 ■ Open 10am–4pm Wed–Sun ■ www.maritime.org

Located inside a 1939 bathhouse, this museum is awash with ship models, figureheads, maritime paintings, and seagoing relics including scrimshaw.

TOP 10 LESSER-KNOWN MUSEUMS

Interior of the Cable Car Museum

1 Cable Car Museum
MAP M3 ■ 1201 Mason St
Located inside a cable barn, this free museum traces the history of the city's iconic transit system.

2 GLBT Historical Society Museum
MAP E5 ■ 4127 18th St
This museum curates stories of the LGBTQ+ community in the city.

3 SFO Museum
San Francisco International Airport
The country's only accredited museum in an airport houses dozens of exhibits throughout its terminals.

4 Pier 24
This massive photography exhibition space (see p63) is free to visit.

5 Pacific Pinball Museum
1510 Webster St, Alameda
Play on 90 pinball machines spanning decades at this interactive museum.

6 The American Bookbinders Museum
MAP G3 ■ 355 Clementina St
This is North America's only museum dedicated to the history of bookbinding.

7 David Ireland House
MAP F5 ■ 500 Capp St
Take a guided tour through the workspace and home of the late artist.

8 Walt Disney Family Museum
MAP D2 ■ 104 Montgomery St, Presidio
This whimsical museum tells the history of the man behind the Disney empire.

9 Tenderloin Museum
MAP Q3 ■ 398 Eddy St
Learn about the rich history of San Francisco's most colorful neighborhood.

10 Wells Fargo History Museum
MAP N5 ■ 420 Montgomery
Observe relics such as gold nuggets at this free banking museum.

⏱ Art Galleries

① City Art Gallery
Owned and operated by the artists themselves, this cooperative gallery *(see p112)* prides itself on making artwork accessible as well as affordable to those interested in collecting or gifting art. Showcasing the work of around 200 local artists – some new, some known and established – the gallery exhibits an array of styles and media through changing exhibitions. Eighty per cent of any sale goes directly to the artist.

② Fraenkel Gallery
MAP P4 ■ 49 Geary St ■ (415) 981-2661 ■ Open 10:30am–5:30pm Tue–Fri, 11am–5pm Sat ■ www.fraenkelgallery.com

Opened in 1979, the gallery held an exhibition early on featuring NASA's lunar photographs, and this set the tone for what followed. Soon came exhibitions by Eugene Atget, Edward Weston, Hiroshi Sugimoto, and Diane Arbus, and later, the Bechers, Adam Fuss, and Sol LeWitt. Projects have brought together work across a variety of media, juxtaposing photography with painting, drawing, and sculpture. Other photographers whose work is regularly showcased include Richard Avedon and Man Ray.

③ Pacific Heritage Museum
MAP N5 ■ 608 Commercial St ■ (415) 399-1124 ■ Open 10am–4pm Tue–Sat

Occupying the historic US Sub-Treasury building from 1875, on top of which the East West Bank has been built. The bank sponsors the museum, which focuses on the art of the Pacific Rim, aiming to bring the work of Asian artists to a wider audience. Exhibitions feature many pieces on loan from private collections.

④ SOMArts Cultural Center
MAP G4 ■ 934 Brannan St between 8th & 9th Sts ■ (415) 863-1414 ■ Open noon–7pm Tue–Fri (to 5pm Sat) ■ www.somarts.org

Group and solo shows, music, and readings all take place here. Founded in 1975, SOMArts is a city-owned cultural center with two exhibition spaces, a 250-seat theater, and printmaking, photography, and design studios.

⑤ Gallery Wendi Norris
MAP F4 ■ 8 Octavia St ■ (415) 346-7812 ■ Open 11am–6pm Tue–Sat ■ www.gallerywendi norris.com

This dynamic and extremely stylish contemporary art venue in South of Market hosts exhibitions of celebrated American and international works, including those by prominent artists from China, Japan, South Korea, and Russia. Some Bay Area artists are also featured

Exterior view of Fraenkel Gallery

in the gallery. The staff is on hand to provide advice to amateur and serious collectors alike about the contemporary art market.

Visitors at 111 Minna Gallery

6 111 Minna Gallery
MAP P5 ▪ 111 Minna St ▪ (415) 974-1719 ▪ Open 7am–9pm Mon–Fri ▪ www.111minnagallery.com

A SoMa district institution since 1993, 111 Minna turns gallery-going into a social event. Visitors can make use of a full bar set within the exhibition space. The gallery features notable local and international artists, and also hosts live performance events.

7 Museo Italo Americano
MAP F1 ▪ Fort Mason Center, Building C ▪ (415) 673-2200 ▪ Open noon–4pm Tue–Sat (Mon by appointment only) ▪ www.museo italoamericano.org

A museum, gallery, and community center for San Francisco's Italians. Regular changing exhibitions might focus on the work of either an individual Italian artist, or on aspects of Italian culture. Classes are also offered at the center on Italian art history, culture, architecture, and cookery.

8 Galería de la Raza
MAP G5 ▪ 2779 Folsom St ▪ (415) 826-8009 ▪ Open noon–6pm Wed–Sat (to 5pm Sun) ▪ www.galeriadelaraza.org

Since its inception in 1970, this gallery has grown to become one of the most respected Latin American arts organizations in the country. It promotes awareness and appreciation of Latin American/Chicano art including painting, photography, and sculpture. Galeria de la Raza also acts as a platform for the performing arts, spoken word nights, as well as projecting digital murals on the building's facade.

9 Berggruen Gallery
MAP Q5 ▪ 10 Hawthorne St ▪ (415) 781-4629 ▪ Open 10am–5pm Mon–Fri, 11am–5pm Sat ▪ www.berggruen.com

One of the most popular galleries for the exhibition and sale of modern American and European art since the 70s. Their displays have included artworks from masters such as de Kooning, Calder, and Matisse.

10 San Francisco Arts Commission Gallery
MAP R1 ▪ 401 Van Ness Ave ▪ (415) 252-2244 ▪ Open noon–5pm Wed–Sat ▪ www.sfartscommission.org/gallery

Opened in 1970, this was one of the first galleries dedicated to showing the work of emerging Bay Area artists. In addition, the Gallery Slide Registry contains images by more than 500 professional artists from across the US.

■10 Writers and Notable Residents

"Beat" author Jack Kerouac

1 Jack Kerouac

Arriving from New York in 1947, it was Kerouac (1922–69) who coined the term "Beat." He and his companions – Neal Cassady, Allen Ginsberg, Lawrence Ferlinghetti, and others – initiated the new politics of dissent and free love that led, within a decade, to the hippie movement *(see p43)*. His novel *On the Road* (1957) galvanized a generation.

2 Isabel Allende

One of the world's most widely read Spanish-language authors, this Chilean American Bay Area resident is famous for her magic realism in *The House of the Spirits*, *City of the Beasts*, *Eva Luna*, and *Of Love and Shadows*. She received the Presidential Medal of Freedom in 2014.

3 Robin Williams

A resident of the Bay Area from when he was a teenager, TV and movie star Williams (1951–2014) began his career as a stand-up comedian in San Francisco clubs and was credited with kick-starting the comedy "renaissance" of the 1970s. Beloved by and friendly to locals, he was known for his generosity to Bay Area charities.

4 William Randolph Hearst

An animated publisher of the *San Francisco Examiner* who built the nation's largest newspaper chain in the late 1800s, Hearst (1863–1951) influenced the American press with his "yellow journalism" tactics, built Hearst Castle, served twice in the House of Representatives, and inspired the movie *Citizen Kane*.

5 Francis Ford Coppola

The director of *The Godfather* makes San Francisco the home of his American Zoetrope productions, and has also branched out into other enterprises. His Inglenook winery in the Napa Valley is one of the best.

6 Jack London

Adventurer and author of frontier tales such as *White Fang*, *The Sea Wolf*, and *The Call of the Wild*, Jack London (1876–1916) grew up in Oakland. A museum of his memorabilia is now housed there, in a recon-struction of the log cabin he lived in while pros-pecting for gold in the Yukon territory. His fiction is based on his experiences in the untamed West and the social inequality he saw in boomtown San Francisco.

Jack London statue in Oakland

7 Dashiell Hammett

The author of *The Maltese Falcon* and creator of the classic hard-boiled detective Sam Spade lived in San Francisco from 1921 to 1929. He used the fog-swirled slopes of the hills as the backdrop for his crime stories. Hammett (1894–1961) was himself employed briefly at the famous Pinkerton Detective Agency.

8 Armistead Maupin

Maupin's *Tales of the City* were serialized in the *San Francisco Chronicle* before being published in book form. They are lighthearted paeans to the lifestyle of LGBTQ+ San Francisco in the 1970s.

9 Carlos Santana

A Mexican American who grew up in San Francisco and was influenced by Bay Area 1960s jazz and folk musicians, Santana founded a band that pioneered Afro-Latin-blues-rock fusion at the Fillmore West, in other area clubs, and at Woodstock. He went on to top the *Billboard* charts for decades, selling more than 100 million records.

Carlos Santana in concert

10 Joe DiMaggio

DiMaggio (1914–99) was born and began his baseball career in San Francisco. His 56-game hitting streak with the New York Yankees made him a legend. He married Marilyn Monroe in San Francisco.

Baseball player Joe DiMaggio

TOP 10 FIGURES FROM THE 1960s

Renowned poet Maya Angelou

1 Maya Angelou
Born in San Francisco, this poet published her first autobiography to international acclaim in 1969.

2 Janis Joplin
This singer from Texas was the queen of the San Francisco sound, until her death by heroin overdose.

3 Ken Kesey
A powerful, revolutionary writer, his Magic Bus and Trips Festival set the tone for the entire hippie movement.

4 Jerry Garcia
Patriarch of the San Francisco sound, his Grateful Dead band continued to tour until his death in 1995.

5 Mario Savio
The UC Berkeley student launched the Free Speech Movement on the campus in the late 1960s.

6 Grace Slick
A quintessentially San Franciscan voice, Slick fronted Jefferson Airplane.

7 Huey Newton
Oakland's founder of the Black Panthers, a group committed to civic and social change.

8 Patty Hearst
The newspaper heiress, kidnapped by the Symbionese Liberation Army in 1974, was apparently converted and took part in an armed robbery.

9 Joan Didion
A native Californian, Didion captured the mood of a generation and the counter-culture of the 1960s in her 1968 book *Slouching Towards Bethlehem*.

10 José Sarria
This influential drag queen became the first openly gay person to run for public office in 1961.

🔟 Parks and Gardens

1 Marina Green
MAP E1

Within sight of the Golden Gate Bridge, and across the street from photogenic 1930s mansions and the Palace of Fine Arts, are several blocks of bayside greensward, which are perfect for picnicking and people-watching. On weekends, observe kite-flyers, joggers, and cyclists, as well as yoga, tai chi, and Zumba practitioners. Some people work out on the seven-station fitness circuit.

2 Alta Plaza
MAP E2

This double block of verdant hill in Pacific Heights is a popular place to sit in the sun when it ventures to break through the fog. Basketball and tennis courts and a children's playground are in the center, while to the south there are terraced lawns, onto which face some of the oldest homes in Pacific Heights.

3 Fort Mason
MAP F1

The rolling lawn above Fort Mason Center (see p99), known as the Great Meadow, is a relatively little-used park, but it's great for taking a siesta, tossing a frisbee, or just strolling through to take in the spectacular views from the cliffs.

4 The Presidio
This vast swath of greenery (see pp98–9) only entered the city's parklands in 1994. It is a beautiful space, and tourists and locals alike come to enjoy the wooded areas, walking trails, and wonderful views over the Bay. It is also home to chic restaurants and museums (see p44). Filmmaker George Lucas created a $350 million headquarters here for his production company Lucasfilm with up to 1,500 employees.

The Conservatory of Flowers

5 Conservatory of Flowers
Shipped around Cape Horn from England and erected in Golden Gate Park in 1879, this magnificent five-story Victorian greenhouse (see p24) contains a jungle of trees, palms, aquatic plants, and flowers. There are thousands of orchids, an enchanting butterfly enclosure, and lily ponds. Plant lovers come from around the world to learn about endangered flora and horticultural innovations like aquascaping.

Aerial view of The Presidio

6 Golden Gate Park

One of the largest city parks in the US is also one of the most diverse, and all of it was brought forth from what was once scrub and dunes. The park also features first-rate cultural attractions such as the de Young Museum (see pp28–9).

7 Lafayette Park
MAP F2

This is another of the double-blocked hilltop gardens in Pacific Heights – a leafy green haven of pine and eucalyptus trees. Steep stairways lead to the summit of the park (see p65), which has delightful views.

8 Rincon Park
MAP H2

Situated just south of the Ferry Building Marketplace on the Embarcadero pedestrian promenade, *Cupid's Span*, a 60-ft- (18-m-) tall sculpture of a red-feathered bow and arrow, marks the location of this bayside park. The lawns and benches afford awesome views of the San Francisco–Oakland Bay Bridge, the city's spectacular skyline, and passing ships.

9 Yerba Buena Gardens

In the South of Market museum district, surrounding the Yerba Buena Center (see pp34–5) for the Arts, are lawns,

Esplanade at the Yerba Buena Gardens

shade trees, gardens, and water features, which create a verdant setting for whimsical outdoor sculptures. Don't miss the 50-ft- (15-m-) wide Martin Luther King, Jr. waterfall.

10 Sigmund Stern Recreation Grove

Famous for its free summer concerts, Sigmund Stern Recreation Grove (see p118) is a leafy recreation complex containing playing fields, tennis and croquet courts, as well as a playground, and a dog park. Pine Lake is popular for jogging, and there are plenty of good picnic spots under the eucalyptus, redwood, and pine trees.

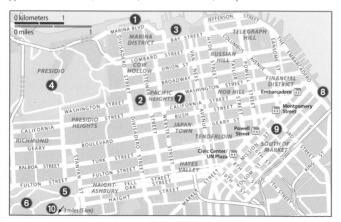

🔟 Beaches

The crescent-shaped Stinson Beach

1 Stinson Beach

Three miles (5 km) of sand (see pp126–7), coupled with the fact that Marin County often has fine weather when the rest of the coast is covered in fog, make this one of the most popular beaches in the Bay Area. It can be busy when it's sunny.

2 Muir and Red Rock Beaches

Muir Beach: off Hwy 1 on Pacific Way ■ Red Rock: 5.5 miles (9 km) north of Muir on Pacific Way

These two beaches, just south of Stinson, are the most famous nude beaches north of San Francisco. Both are sandy curves within their own coves, protected from wind and prying eyes by rocky cliffs. The only caveat is that you'll need

The rocky cliffs overlooking Muir Beach

sturdy walking shoes to get down the rough paths that lead to them from the parking lots.

3 China Beach
MAP B2

This is the poshest beach in San Francisco, being adjacent to the exclusive Sea Cliff neighborhood. Despite its pedigree, California law requires that all coastal areas remain public, although access roads to them can be private. China Beach is small and protected from the wind, there's plenty of parking, and it's a pleasant walk to the sand. You'll find showers and changing rooms, as well as grills and picnic areas here.

4 Pacifica Beaches
Hwy 1

A 20-minute drive south of the city are several Pacific Ocean beaches popular with surfers, swimmers, and families. A favorite of beginner surfers, Linda Mar Beach has rest-rooms and showers, and connects by a breezy trail to Rockaway Beach. Sharp Park Beach has picnic sites, a fishing pier with a café, parking, and nature trails.

5 Bolinas Beach

This hidden-away Marin beach (see p127) tends to be windy and is mostly used by dog-walkers and kayakers. It's sandy, with a backdrop of rocky cliffs. If you walk north, you'll find sheltered nooks, where some sun-worshippers bask in the nude, although there is a rarely enforced city ordinance against it.

The Golden Gate Bridge viewed from Baker Beach

6 Baker Beach
MAP C2

This 1-mile (1.5-km) stretch of sandy beach, with its perfect views of the Golden Gate Bridge, is the most popular in the city. It's great for sunbathing, dog-walking, picnicking, or jogging, but signs warn off swimmers because of riptides. The sunsets here are unforgettable.

7 Ocean Beach

Some 4 miles (6.5 km) long and quite broad, this is the city's largest beach by far *(see p117)*, but probably the worst for entering the water safely. It starts at Cliff House and continues on beyond the city limits, turning into picturesque dunes at the southern end. Great for walking or jogging, and when the sun comes out, it's a fine place to sunbathe.

8 Marshall's Beach
MAP C1

Also known as Land's End Beach, Marshall's Beach is secluded almost beneath the Golden Gate Bridge, with stunning sea views and good sightings of seabirds. A clothing optional beach, Marshall's is popular with open-minded locals and the city's LGBTQ+ residents. Access is via the steep Batteries to Bluffs Trail, or from popular North Baker Beach, also a nude beach. Swimming is prohibited due to strong currents.

9 Aquatic Park

Shielded by a fishing pier shaped like a horseshoe, this *(see p98)* is a human-made lagoon near Fisherman's Wharf, with a sandy beach, a seawall for lounging, restrooms, and a walkway making it accessible to wheelchairs and bikes. This is the number-one spot from which to watch the Fourth of July fireworks. Sometimes swimming is prohibited due to water quality.

10 East Beach
MAP D1

On the paved Bay Trail between the yacht harbor in the Marina District and Crissy Field, with dazzling Golden Gate Bridge and Alcatraz views, this is one of the only beaches where swimming is safe from undertows and currents. On site are picnic tables and grills, restrooms, lawns for lounging, and free parking.

🔟 Outdoor Activities

A hiking trail on Mount Tamalpais

regattas and boating events, from Opening Day on the Bay to Fleet Week and the Fourth of July.

④ Skating

It's great fun to watch inline and roller skaters show off their skills. They also offer lessons from noon to 5pm on Sundays at 5th Avenue and Kennedy Drive in Golden Gate Park. Skating can also be enjoyed on the paved path at Marina Green.

① Hiking

The Bay Area is replete with hiking trails for nature-lovers. Land's End offers wild terrain to scramble over (see p119), and Mount Tamalpais is crisscrossed with trails (see p126), but just scaling the city's hills is enough hiking for most people.

② Swimming

Embarcadero YMCA: MAP H2; 169 Steuart St; (415) 957-9622; www. ymcasf.org

Some hotels and the Embarcadero YMCA have pools, and close-to-shore swimming can be enjoyed at a few spots, namely China Beach, the protected cove at Aquatic Park, and the shallow waters off Crissy Field – kids wade in the tidal marsh here, too.

③ Sailing

OCSC Sailing School: www. ocscsailing.com

Charter a yacht or a masted schooner, take sailing lessons, or tour the Bay on a motor cruiser, catamaran, or sailboat. Fun to watch are the frequent

⑤ Running

Bay to Breakers: open 3rd Sun in May; (415) 231-3130; ■ San Francisco Marathon: open Jun or Jul; (888) 958-6668; www. thesfmarathon.com

Since the restoration of Crissy Field, the Golden Gate Promenade (see p98) has been an inspiring run – and, of course, Golden Gate Park offers endless opportunities for jogging. If organized running is your thing, try the Bay to Breakers or the San Francisco Marathon.

⑥ Tennis

San Francisco Recreation and Park Department: www.sfrecpark.org ■ Golden Gate Park: (415) 753-7001

Visit the website of the Recreation and Park department to reserve a time slot at a public tennis court for free. Golden Gate Park courts charge a small fee; book in advance. Most public out-door courts are open from sunrise to sunset. Indoor courts are the purview of private tennis clubs, with membership required.

Sailing in the Bay

7 Golf

Golden Gate Park: (415) 751-8987 ■ **Lincoln Park: (415) 221-9911** ■ **Presidio Golf Course: (415) 561-4661** ■ **TPC Harding Park: (415) 664-4690**

TPC Harding Park has been revamped for professional tournaments, and Presidio Golf Course is among the best in the country. Locals love Lincoln Park, an affordable course above Land's End; the par 3 Golden Gate Park Golf Course; and the nine-hole Gleneagles Golf Course.

Biking near the Golden Gate Bridge

8 Biking

City Cycle: 3001 Steiner St; (415) 346-2242; www.citycycle.com

Cycling is big in San Francisco. Don't miss biking across the Golden Gate Bridge. Rent bikes from City Cycle.

9 Kayaking

San Francisco Kayak & Adventures: Pier 52; (415) 787-2628; www.sfkayak.com

Unpredictable waters and winds in the Bay call for a professional guide. While sunset paddle tours are available at Richardson Bay and Angel Island, you can enjoy a calmer experience at McCovey Cove.

10 Windsurfing

The Bay is one of the most popular windsurfing and kiteboarding sites in the world. Spectators often watch from the shoreline, especially at Crissie Field. Boardsports shops offer lessons and rentals.

TOP 10 SPORTING TEAMS

Levi's Stadium, home of the 49ers

1 San Francisco 49ers
4900 Marie P. DeBartolo Way, Santa Clara ■ (415) 656-4900
NFL team, plays September to January.

2 San Francisco Giants
Oracle Park, 24 Willie Mays Plaza ■ (415) 972-2000
Baseball team, plays April to October.

3 Golden State Warriors
Chase Center, 1 Warriors Way ■ (888) 479-4667
An NBA basketball team.

4 Oakland Athletics
(510) 638-4900
Historic winners of Major League Baseball in the 1970s.

5 San Jose Earthquakes
Avaya Stadium, 1123 Coleman Ave, San Jose ■ (408) 556-7700
Men's Major League Soccer team.

6 The San Jose Barracuda
525 W Santa Clara St, San Jose ■ (408) 287-7070
Professional ice hockey team in the American Hockey League.

7 Napa Valley 1839 FC
1400 Menlo Ave, Napa
Wine Country-based men's soccer club that competes in the National Premier Soccer League Golden Gate Conference.

8 The San Jose Spiders
12345 El Monte Rd, Los Altos Hills ■ www.theaudl.com/spiders
Ultimate frisbee team based in San Jose.

9 San Jose Sharks
SAP Center, 525 West Santa Clara St, San Jose ■ www.nhl.com/sharks
Fast-paced NHL ice hockey.

10 Sacramento Kings
Golden 1 Center Arena, 547 L St, Sacramento ■ www.nba.com/kings
Men's NBA basketball team.

🔟 Off the Beaten Path

The Lyon Street steps, leading into the verdant Presidio

1 Lyon Street Steps
MAP E2 ■ Lyon St at Broadway

Take your time climbing the Lyon Street steps adjacent to the Presidio (there are over 200) for sweeping, bird's-eye views of the Bay, the Presidio, the Palace of Fine Arts, and the manicured gardens and balconied perfection of the Pacific Heights mansions. At the top there is a gate into the Presidio.

2 Tin How Temple
MAP N4 ■ 125 Waverly Place ■ Open 10am–4pm daily

On a Chinatown backstreet in a colorful 19th-century building, a narrow stairway leads past a mah-jongg parlor to the Tin How Temple, where incense wafts through a lantern-lit chamber dedicated to the Queen of Heaven. Be respectful, and burn a joss stick for your fortune.

3 Angel Island State Park
Belvedere Tiburon ■ Café: opening hours vary, check website ■ www.angelisland.com

Live music and draft beer make the deck at Angel Island Café a good place to hang out on week-ends. Catch the ferry from Tiburon (see website for details) and head for the picnic tables on the lawns around Ayala Cove where sailboats, kayaks, and power yachts come and go. Walking and biking trails connect historic sites and a secluded beach.

4 Free SF Tour
MAP E5 ■ 389 Post St (corner of Powell) ■ https://freesftour.com

This local company offers a variety of walking tours that explore many parts of the city. The Downtown night tour traverses Union Square, the Embarcadero, Chinatown, and the Financial District, giving walkers a local-like perspective of San Francisco. Though the tour is free, attendees are encouraged to tip the guides – all of whom are volunteers.

The SS *Jeremiah O'Brien* Liberty Ship

5 SS Jeremiah O'Brien
Ferrying troops and supplies during World War II, the SS *Jeremiah O'Brien (see p17)* is one of only two restored survivors of the original 2,710 Liberty Ships. It also took part in the invasion of Normandy. Located on Pier 45, this 441-ft- (134-m-) long ship fires up her engines on "Steaming Weekends" and there are daily tours as well.

6 Pier 24
The Embarcadero, below the Bay Bridge ■ (415) 512-7424 ■ **Open 9am–5:15pm Mon–Fri (by appointment)** ■ www.pier24.org

Once an industrial space, this facility *(see p51)* now houses an incredible photography exhibition gallery, mostly featuring the works of renowned American photographers. Entry is free but reservations must be made in advance on Pier 24's website.

7 Gospel Music at Glide Memorial Church

Crowds gather on Sundays at 9am and 11am for the joyful noise of services at Glide Memorial United Methodist Church *(see p46)*. With a 125-voice gospel choir singing jazz, blues, and rock and roll, plus an audience made up of all ages, races, and religions, the emotional scene is set for the compelling Marvin K. White, who welcomes all comers.

8 Yachting and Lawn Bowling in the Park
MAP B4 ■ **Golden Gate Park** ■ (415) 386-1037 ■ **Open 1–4pm daily & for events** ■ **Model Yacht Club: www.sfmyc.org** ■ **Lawn Bowling Club: www.sflbc.org**

For more than a century, members of the Lawn Bowling Club have welcomed spectators at their greensward. The steam-powered and electric sailing vessels of the Model Yacht Club can be seen zooming across Spreckels Lake daily, particularly during the Wooden Boats on Parade event held every second year in October.

Lawn Bowling Club, Golden Gate Park

9 Cottage Row
MAP F3 ■ **Between Sutter & Bush** ■ (415) 391-2000 ■ **Open sunrise–sunset**

The hidden gem of Cottage Row Historic District is lined with late 1800s Italianate houses from the days of horse-drawn streetcars. Around the corner are the "Painted Ladies" – elaborate Victorian houses.

10 Presidio Sculptures
MAP D2 ■ www.presidio.gov

Sculptures by Andy Goldsworthy are set in the Presidio forest. His 100-ft-(30-m-) high *Spire*, made of cypress trees, towers in a copse. *Wood Line* is in century-old eucalyptus groves.

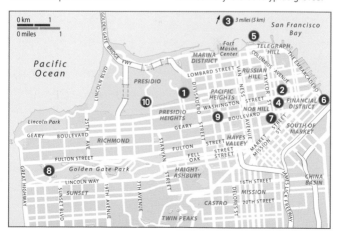

🔟 Children's Attractions

Children's Creativity Museum, Yerba Buena Gardens

1 Children's Creativity Museum

This elaborate complex *(see p34)*, is part of the Yerba Buena Gardens. There's a carousel; a labyrinth; a studio where kids can script, produce, and star in their own videos; art studios; and a digital workshop. Suitable for those aged 2 to 12.

2 San Francisco Zoo

Kids will never forget their direct encounters with farm animals at the zoo *(see p119)* and visits with animal babies, which may include gorillas, snow leopards, rhinos, or alpacas. Top-quality children's programs, many feeding times and the creepy-crawly insect denizens, make it a must for budding zoologists.

3 Aquariums

Part of Golden Gate Park's California Academy of Sciences *(see pp26–7)*, the Steinhart Aquarium is a big hit with kids. The darkened corridors are filled with glowing tanks, home to some of the weirdest creatures on the planet. There's also the Touching Tidal Pool that allows kids to get up close to their finny friends. At Fisherman's Wharf *(see p16)*, Aquarium of the Bay gives an even greater under-sea experience, with walk-through transparent tunnels surrounded by sea life.

4 Randall Museum

MAP E4 ■ 199 Museum Way, off Roosevelt Way, Buena Vista ■ (415) 554-9600 ■ Open 10am–5pm Tue–Sat ■ Closed Mon and public hols ■ www. randallmuseum.org

A small, welcoming complex, this museum has plenty of animals in the petting zoo, honeybees, a model train, a Natural Sciences Lab, ceramic studio, and a high-tech STEM lab. There are also interactive desert, riparian, urban, and marine habitats.

5 Alcatraz

"The Rock" *(see pp18–21)* is always a hit with older children, particularly those who enjoy the grim aspects of the place. The island's natural beauty, as well as the ferry ride out and back, will also delight.

6 Bay Area Discovery Museum

557 McReynolds Rd, Sausalito ■ (415) 339-3900 ■ Open 10am–4pm, Wed–Sun ■ Closed public hols & last two weeks in Sep ■ Adm ■ www. bayareadiscoverymuseum.org

This hands-on museum on the Marin waterfront is aimed at children aged 6 months to 10 years. There's an art studio, a science lab, a wave workshop, and a media center. There are year-round day camps as well.

(7) Metreon

Intended as a high-tech, multilevel amusement arcade for adolescents, this shopping centre *(see p34)* has an impressive IMAX 3D movie theater. Here, you can watch the latest Hollywood blockbusters with sound effects amped up to the highest level. The Metreon also offers several restaurant choices and great views over the city from the fourth-floor deck.

(8) Children's Fairyland

699 Bellevue Ave, Oakland
■ (510) 452-2259 ■ Open Wed–Sun (hours vary) ■ www.fairyland.org
Opened in 1948, this amusement park was the inspiration for Disneyland. It was designed for ages 8 years and under and only admits adults accompanied by children.

(9) Angel Island State Park

Angel Island *(see p96)* is ideal for a full-day family outing. You can picnic, swim, hike, kayak, camp, or take the tram tour that goes around the island, with a guide who points out sites of historic interest.

(10) Exploratorium

At this science museum *(see p88)* kids can learn how their senses work, and also delve into the laws of physics through first-hand experiments, like making simple circuit boards. Reserve in advance (additional fee) for the Tactile Dome, in which you feel your way along in total darkness.

Making circuit boards, Exploratorium

Helen Diller Civic Center

TOP 10 PLAYGROUNDS

1 Helen Diller Civic Center Playground
MAP R2 ■ 55 Larkin St
An award-winning playscape inspired by the city's weather patterns.

2 Sue Bierman Park
MAP N6 ■ Washington St and Drumm St
This pirate-themed playground is a roosting spot for the city's feral parrots.

3 Willie "Woo Woo" Wong Playground
MAP N4 ■ 830 Sacramento St
Named after a local basketball star, this urban park features sand-floor grounds.

4 Golden Gate Park 45th Avenue Playground
Part of the larger park *(see p57)*, this ground has ocean-themed structures.

5 Lafayette Park
Dog-friendly park *(see p57)* with tennis courts and hilltop views of the city.

6 Joe DiMaggio Playground
MAP L3 ■ 651 Lombard St
North Beach park with athletic and bocce courts and large play structures.

7 Huntington Park
MAP N3 ■ California St and Taylor St
Atop posh Nob Hill, this park includes a stately fountain and a play area.

8 Alta Plaza Park
MAP E2 ■ Jackson St and Steiner St
Concrete staircases crisscross this hilltop park and playground *(see p56)*.

9 Presidio Wall Playground
MAP D2 ■ Pacific St and Spruce St
With jungle gyms, a slide and ball fields, this park has everything for a day out.

10 South Park
MAP H3 ■ 64 S Park St
This park has a play structure inspired by designer Isamu Noguchi.

TOP 10 Performing Arts Venues

War Memorial Opera House and San Francisco Ballet

1 War Memorial Opera House and San Francisco Ballet

MAP R1 ■ 301 Van Ness Ave
■ www.sfopera.com

The San Francisco Opera Company is one of the largest in the country and performs here for some of the year. The excellent San Francisco Ballet, one of the nation's oldest ballet companies, mostly performs at the War Memorial Opera House.

2 Louise M. Davies Symphony Hall

MAP R1 ■ 201 Van Ness Ave ■ (415) 864-6000 ■ www.sfsymphony.org

With performances from September through to May, the San Francisco Symphony Orchestra performs in this glass-fronted structure with its carefully modulated acoustics. Look out for the Henry Moore bronze sculpture out front. World-famous artists, orchestras and conductors from all around the globe can be found on the program, along with holiday productions.

3 Masonic Auditorium

MAP N3 ■ 1111 California St ■ (415) 776-7457
■ www.sfmasonic.com

Originally a Masonic Temple, built in 1957, this attractive structure, with its 3,300-seat auditorium, is used as a venue for lectures, and readings, jazz performances, as well as conventions and seminars. The mosaics depict some of the tenets of Freemasonry. Do not miss the sculpture on the outside of the building, created by Emile Norman.

4 Curran Theater

MAP P3 ■ 445 Geary St ■ (415) 358-1220 ■ www.sfcurran.com

After the renovation of its grand 1922 structure in 2017, the Curran now houses a range of productions, from the *Bright Star* bluegrass musical by Steve Martin, to edgy *Fun Home*, a musical about the coming of age in the LGBTQ+ community. Three glamorous new bars add to the ambiance.

5 The Fillmore

MAP E3 ■ 1805 Geary St ■ (415) 346-6000
■ www.the fillmore.com

Originally named the Majestic Hall, this legendary music hall *(see p45)* became the
Fillmore Auditorium in 1954. Since then, it has hosted many San Francisco greats, including Jimmy Hendrix, Janis Joplin, the Grateful Dead, and still showcases the finest touring rock and pop acts

Conor Oberst at The Fillmore

in the world. Be sure to check out the historic collection of concert posters on the mezzanine level.

6 Orpheum Theatre
MAP R2 ■ 1192 Market St
■ (888) 746-1799 ■ www.orpheum
theatersanfrancisco.org

Originally a vaudeville house and then a movie theater, this is the historic spot where *Hair* was given its first West Coast performance some 30 years ago – known locally as "the New York version of what happened here in San Francisco." Concerts and theater performances range from Billy Joel and Bruno Mars to *The Lion King* and *Les Miserables*.

Facade of the Orpheum Theatre

7 SFJAZZ Center
MAP R1 ■ 201 Franklin St at Fell St ■ (866) 920-5299 ■ www.sfjazz.org

With specially designed acoustics and an intimate concert hall, the building that houses the SFJAZZ Center is the first in the US to be specifically built for jazz performances. The center aims to educate and inspire audiences with an eclectic program of events from world-class musicians.

8 Golden Gate Theatre
MAP Q3 ■ 1 Taylor St
■ (888) 746-1799 ■ www.shnsf.com

This former movie house, designed with Moorish influences in the 1920s, is one of the city's larger mainstream theaters. Its usual offerings are traveling Broadway blockbusters, such as *Aladdin*, *The Book of Mormon*, and *Waitress*.

9 American Conservatory Theater (ACT)
MAP P3 ■ The Toni Rembe Theater, 405 Geary St ■ (415) 749-2228
■ www.act-sf.org

Founded in the 1960s, San Francisco's most important theater company is internationally respected and has produced premieres of a number of major plays. At the heart of ACT is one of the most acclaimed actor-training institutions in the nation. Its former students include Annette Bening and Denzel Washington.

10 Magic Theatre
MAP F1 ■ Fort Mason Center, Building D ■ (415) 441-8822 ■ www. magictheatre.org

In the 1970s, none other than Sam Shepard was the resident playwright of the Magic, and its stage has seen performances by the likes of Sean Penn and Nick Nolte. It specializes in new plays, usually by up-and-coming Americans, and also offers "raw play" readings of as yet unstaged works.

TOP 10 Nightlife

The Tonga Room and Hurricane Bar offer a South Sea Island theme

1 The Tonga Room and Hurricane Bar

This Nob Hill tiki bar *(see p92)* is almost Disneyesque in its tropical effects, including indoor monsoons and a floating band. Aimed at grown-ups of every age, it has delivered kitschy Polynesian dazzlement since 1945, and is often chosen as the venue for birthday celebrations. There is a live band, and an entertainment surcharge of $15 per person is charged after 7pm (regardless of arrival time).

2 The Great Northern

One of the few venues in San Francisco which is large enough to be considered a proper dance club, The Great Northern *(see p113)* is well known for its fun hip-hop shows and international house DJs. It is beloved by club-goers for its great variety of music, its size, and its revolving art collection.

3 DNA Lounge

Situated in the SoMa district, the eclectic, sprawling DNA Lounge *(see p114)* features seven bars, four dance floors, and two stages. Patrons can enjoy everything from storytelling events to burlesque shows and DJ sets. The full-service restaurant here serves food until late at night.

4 Bottom of the Hill

Open seven days a week in Potrero Hill, this is one of the best live-music venues in a city that is renowned for its live music. Even though Bottom of the Hill *(see p114)* has a definite punk vibe, you are just as likely to hear a folk music act playing as a hard-core punk band. If you don't care for the music, just head to the back where you can grab a table out of earshot.

5 Boom Boom Room

MAP F3 ■ 1601 Fillmore St
■ www.boomboomroom.com

The Filmore district of the past is sometimes called "the Harlem of

Vibrant exterior of Boom Boom Room

the West", a place where jazz legends like Billie Holiday, Miles Davis, and Dexter Gordon could be heard. This era is past, but the Boom Boom Room remains popular for its great live blues, jazz, and funk music, and for its welcoming mood, friendly staff and great energy.

Live performance at Bimbo's 365 Club

6 Monarch
MAP G3 ■ 101 6th St
■ www.monarchsf.com

Known for attracting some of San Francisco's best bands, Monarch is a premier nightclub nestled in the Theater District. It's a multifunctional space, which can equally serve an evening of high-brow lounging and craft cocktail tasting, as well as a night of house music and disco beats.

7 The Hidden Vine
A classy, cozy wine bar *(see p92)*, The Hidden Vine offers a selection of close to 180 types of wine from all over the world. The diverse food menu contains specialties such as cheese charcuterie platters, as well as organic, seasonal tapas. A different wine region is featured every month. The Vine has also been ranked as one of the top ten wine bars in America by *USA Today*. If visiting with a large group, reserve the *bocce* court.

8 Make-Out Room
Popularly known as Mission's favorite nightclub *(see p113)*, the Make-Out Room has live music, comedy, and literary events. The fun atmosphere is enhanced by the witty and friendly staff. They offer happy hours every night.

9 Bimbo's 365 Club
Whether you are into swing, jazz, or rock, this San Francisco institution *(see p92)* delivers. A retro-chic yet unpretentious music venue that was established in 1931, this excellent hopping bar with glittering decor and an old-school feel brings in all the top acts to entertain. Their old-fashioned New Year's Eve parties are legendary.

10 Punch Line Comedy Club
An alternative to bar-hopping, there is no better venue for a good laugh than this hilarious comedy club *(see p92)*. Watch national, as well as upcoming local acts, which will headline a fun evening in an intimate setting, with all the seating up close to the stage. Buy tickets in advance to ensure good seats.

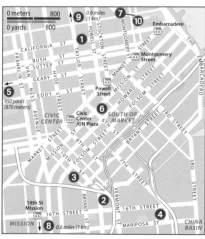

🔟 LGBTQ+ Venues

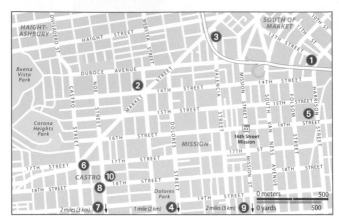

1 SF Eagle
MAP G4 ■ 398 12th St

Bikers and leather boys still rule at this venerable SoMa dive. Come here to revel in the beer-busting, sexually free atmosphere. The back patio gets going on Sunday afternoons, and Thursdays feature performances by local bands.

2 Churchill
MAP F4 ■ 198 Church St ■ (415) 570-9198

Located in the Castro district, this cocktail bar is set in military barracks inspired by those used in World War II. It features vintage artifacts, as well as pool tables, and serves top-notch cocktails in mason jars. It also offers fine wines and a variety of draft and bottled beers.

3 Martuni's
MAP F4 ■ 4 Valencia St at Market ■ (415) 241-0205

With its decor of glass and chrome and the regulars' penchant for singing old torch songs, this is a very retro piano bar for an older LGBTQ+ crowd. It's a magnet for drag queens, mature gay men, heterosexuals, and anyone who likes a good singalong – or who doesn't mind embarrassing themselves on the microphone.

4 El Rio
MAP F6 ■ 3158 Mission St (at Cesar Chavez) ■ (415) 282-3325 ■ www.elriosf.com

A delightful dive bar that features daily specials on drinks and free

Guests eating at El Rio

oysters on Fridays, and occasionally hosts live events. There are plenty of other activities too, including shuffleboard, pool, and ping pong tables on the back patio. Carry some cash if you plan on visiting over the weekend as cards may not be accepted.

5 Jolene's
MAP G4 ▪ 2700 16th St ▪ (415) 621-8579 ▪ www.jolenessf.com

An array of events take place here: Western gear is encouraged on Coyote Queer while Beso! is a queer Latin American party. The venue proudly welcomes the transgender and non-binary communities. On Sundays there is the Drag & Burlesque Variety Show and brunch. Check the website for all the programs at this Mission district favorite.

6 Twin Peaks
MAP E5 ▪ 401 Castro St ▪ (415) 864-9470

Conveniently located on the corner of Market Street, this legendary and distinctive tavern offers one of the best views of the Castro, whether by day or night. The interior is an inviting, pillowed triangular space with plate-glass windows.

Neon sign outside Twin Peaks

7 Wild Side West
MAP G6 ▪ 424 Cortland Ave ▪ (415) 647-3099 ▪ www.wildsidewest.com

Founded in the 1960s, this laid-back spot has a full bar inside, a patio area out back, and a beer garden. Take part in a game of pool or enjoy the flatscreens on game days. Trivia night is every Wednesday at 8pm.

Moby Dick exterior

8 Moby Dick
MAP E5 ▪ 4049 18th St ▪ (415) 861-1199

This old-time Castro hangout attracts a more mature crowd. It's generally a bunch of regulars getting together for pinball or pool. The windows are big, so you can keep track of what's going down on the street. The music is largely 1980s retro, which sets a fun-loving tone.

9 Sundance Saloon
MAP G6 ▪ 550 Barneveld Ave near Hwys 280 and 101 ▪ (415) 820-1403 ▪ www.sundancesaloon.org

Wear your Stetson and boots at this large country-and-western dance club. Two-step and linedance lessons are offered twice weekly. The saloon also hosts various special events.

10 Last Call Bar
MAP E5 ▪ 3988 18th St ▪ (415) 861-1310 ▪ www.thelastcallbar.com

Friendly, unpretentious dive bar with an Irish pub-like atmosphere, complete with a jukebox machine, two large screens that cater to sports fans, and a cozy fireplace to keep warm on cold and foggy days. Happy hour begins at noon and lasts till 7pm every day.

TOP 10 Restaurants

Intimate and modern interior at two-Michelin-starred Quince

1 Quince

Run by Michelin-starred chef Michael Tusk, Quince (see p93) is considered by many to be the best restaurant in the city. It serves dish after dish of beautiful Californian fare, which is influenced by northern Italy, and is prepared with the freshest local ingredients.

2 Trestle

This cozy bistro (see p93) features an affordable, seasonal three-course prix fixe (which comes along with the option to add a pasta course), as well as a key ingredient: San Francisco-style service that is both refined and welcoming.

3 Mourad

Marrakesh-born, Michelin-starred chef Mourad Lahlou adds a contemporary Californian twist to traditional Moroccan cuisine in his eponymously named restaurant (see p93), set in a historic building.

4 A16

Known for its traditional Neapolitan pizzas, fresh pastas, house-cured salami, and regional wines, this casual yet chic marina restaurant (see p101) will transport you straight to southern Italy.

5 Greens

The first fine-dining vegetarian restaurant (see p101) in the city, Annie Sommerville's famous restaurant was inspired by the huge success of the former Zen bakery and coffee shop. The drinks menu only features organic and sustainable wines. This spacious, pleasant Marina restaurant came to define vegetarian cuisine for the Bay Area.

6 Scoma's

Established in 1965, this great seafood spot (see p101) started off as a small coffee shop for fishers. Today, it offers everything from crab bisque to fish and chips. There are gluten-free and vegetarian options available as well. They also feature an extensive wine list.

7 Foreign Cinema

In the courtyard, a selection of old and new movies are projected onto a neighboring building while you dine. The Mediterranean-influenced food here (see p115) is also excellent and the oyster bar and Sunday brunch are popular.

8 Lers Ros Thai
Lers Ros *(see p93)* delivers fresh Thai dishes in a no-frills, casual dining room. Arrive early or you'll be standing in line down the street. Reservations are also available.

9 Delfina
Thanks to its perfect, modern Italian fare made with the freshest local ingredients, it has been hard to get a table at Delfina *(see p115)* for years now, which is saying a lot in a city that has trendy restaurants opening every month. In addition to the legendary chicken and delicate pasta dishes at Delfina, pizza lovers can indulge in the best Neapolitan pizza outside of Italy at its pizzeria next door.

10 Spruce
This Michelin-starred restaurant's *(see p107)* excellent seasonal Nouveau American menu has a major meat focus. For the same delicious food with a slightly less formal feel, opt to sit in the bar area, where you can also enjoy some handcrafted cocktails.

Pastrami sandwich, Spruce

TOP 10 ROMANTIC DINNER SPOTS

Diners outside Chez Panisse

1 Chez Panisse
Established by Alice Waters in 1971, this restaurant *(see p131)* is the birthplace of Cal-Med cuisine. Book weeks ahead.

2 Atelier Crenn
MAP E2 ▪ 3127 Fillmore ▪ (415) 440-0460 ▪ $$$
Delicious food, and the dining room is intimate and quiet.

3 Acquerello
MAP N1 ▪ 1722 Sacramento St ▪ (415) 567-5432 ▪ $$$
An Italian fine-dining establishment offering a wide selection of wines.

4 Chapeau!
Fine French cuisine and exceptional wine at this cozy bistro *(see p123)*.

5 Boulevard
MAP H2 ▪ 1 Mission St ▪ (415) 543-6084 ▪ $$$
Enjoy the *belle époque* decor and superb food here.

6 BIX
MAP M5 ▪ 56 Gold St ▪ (415) 433-6300 ▪ $$$
Stylish spot with retro decor and atmospheric live music.

7 La Mar
MAP M6 ▪ Pier 1.5 Embarcadero at Washington ▪ (415) 397-8880 ▪ $$
Dine in a stunning blue and white dining room looking out over the Bay.

8 Gary Danko
Sophisticated Contemporary cuisine is prepared with carefully selected ingredients here *(see p101)*.

9 Frascati
A cozy bistro *(see p101)* with great views of the cable cars on Hyde Street.

10 Beach Chalet Brewery
A great oceanside spot for dining with sunset views *(see p123)*.

For a key to restaurant price ranges see p93 ←

▓▓ Cafés and Bars

① Specs' Twelve Adler Museum Café

With an exuberant atmosphere *(see p89)*, this bar is like a museum filled with Beat memorabilia. The popular house drink here is the Jack Kerouac, which is a mix of rum, tequila, orange or cranberry juice, and lime.

② Caffè Trieste

If you are interested in learning about the colorful history of this quarter, do not miss out on this North Beach landmark *(see p92)*. Whether it is from the literary and artistic point of view, or for the Italian culture, this place makes for a great experience. It's a great place for a cup of something warm, and to sit and people-watch, or dip into one of San Francisco's free weekly newspapers.

③ Blue Bottle Café

This hip coffee roaster *(see p92)* kicked off San Francisco's latest café trend; it serves up perfect cappuccinos and lattes in its chic, industrial SoMa space. Also on offer are Kyoto-style iced coffees, brewed using the Japanese slow-drip method. Perfection takes time, however, and these baristas take their work very seriously, so be prepared for a bit of a wait. The experience is worth trying at least once.

Slow-drip brewers, Blue Bottle Café

Fresh bread, Tartine Bakery and Café

④ Tartine Bakery and Café

You may find a line out the door at this purveyor of rustic breads *(see p115)*, "hot pressed" sandwiches, pizzas, cakes, and tarts. The co-owners have both been awarded the James Beard Award for Outstanding Pastry Chefs.

⑤ The Buena Vista Café

Established in 1916 at the cable car turnaround at Fisherman's Wharf, The Buena Vista Café *(see p101)* is always packed with customers who come for the good breakfasts and strong coffee. This friendly café claims to have been the first to introduce Irish coffee to America in 1952. First served at Shannon Airport in Ireland, the flavorful drink is composed of Irish whiskey, a sugar cube, hot coffee, and a foamy collar of whipped cream.

⑥ Arizmendi

This cooperative *(see p107)* delights customers on both sides of the bay with artisan breads, delicious morning pastries, and gourmet pizzas. The 9th Ave location is just a block from the Golden Gate Park.

7 One Market

Located just a few steps away from the Embarcadero and the waterfront, this lively bistro *(see p93)* sets an atmosphere for fun. It offers California-style cuisine and the dishes are created out of farm-fresh ingredients.

8 Bourbon & Branch

You'll need the nightly password to enter this classy bar *(see p114)*. Once inside, enjoy inventive cocktails in one of the most beautifully designed bars in the city, and explore the many secret rooms.

9 Vesuvio Café

Since 1948, Vesuvio *(see p92)* has been the North Beach haunt of artists, writers, and bon vivants of all stripes, many of whom wander across the street to the famous City Lights Bookstore *(see p90)* and back.

10 Absinthe

Established in 1988, this bistro *(see p107)* is widely popular with the locals. The menu here offers Parisian-style fare along with a wide selection of classic cocktails. Located adjacent to the bar is a private dining room, with an interior that captures fin-de-siècle France. Make sure to check out their incredible wine list.

Outdoor seating at Absinthe

TOP 10 BRUNCH VENUES

French toast served with fruits

1 Mama's on Washington Square
MAP L4 ▪ 1701 Stockton St
▪ Closed Mon
The greatest French toast in town.

2 Sears Fine Food
This Union Square institution *(see p93)* is noted for its silver dollar pancakes.

3 Plow
MAP H5 ▪ 1299 18th St
Farm-to-table delights such as smoked trout toast and lemon ricotta pancakes.

4 Fable
MAP E5 ▪ 558 Castro St
Enjoy pancakes and French toast with steak, eggs Benedict, and chilaquiles on a sunny patio at this place.

5 Kantine
MAP F4 ▪ 1906 Market St ▪ Closed Mon
Scandinavian-style porridges, pastries and customizable brunch boards.

6 Presidio Social Club
MAP E2 ▪ 563 Ruger St
An elegant restaurant serving up old-school drinks and brunch classics.

7 Just for You Café
MAP H5 ▪ 732 22nd St
Soul food-inspired brunch in the Dogpatch neighborhood.

8 Kate's Kitchen
MAP F4 ▪ 471 Haight St
Huge portions of breakfast specialties, including a "French Toast Orgy."

9 Tosca Café
MAP G2 ▪ 242 Columbus Ave
A good selection of bagels and French toasts topped with fruits.

10 St. Francis Fountain
MAP G5 ▪ 2801 24th St
A charming, classic diner with wooden booths and a candy counter. Serves all-day breakfast.

🔟 Stores and Shopping Centers

Food stalls at the Marketplace

1 Ferry Building Marketplace

Wander through one of the world's greatest gourmet food markets *(see p45)* and stop to taste fresh oysters, Vietnamese or Mexican food, salumi, Blue Bottle coffee, pastries, chocolates, and cheesecake. Visit the outdoor Saturday farmers' market, right in front of the Ferry Building, set along the Embarcadero.

2 Alexander Book Company

This excellent three-level bookstore *(see p112)* offers all kinds of books and periodicals, ranging from classic literature and poetry to cookbooks and romance novels. Do not miss the sidewalk sale before you enter to score some deals on non-fiction or interesting self-help books.

3 Neiman Marcus
MAP P4 ■ 150 Stockton St

After some retail therapy at the designer clothing store, Neiman Marcus, grab a quick bite in the Fresh Market, or linger at The Rotunda for fine dining, or high tea, under the stained-glass dome, while admiring the views.

4 Wilkes Bashford

This luxury clothing store *(see p112)* features high-end designers with a bent for fashionable clothing and footwear. It offers perfect options for the denizens of the Financial District.

5 Amoeba Music

Situated along Haight Street, Amoeba *(see p106)* is the world's largest Indie music store, with several other locations in California. It stocks LPs, tapes, as well as CDs and evokes a true sense of the past. Also on sale here are a vast selection of DVDs, apparel, and posters, and plenty of branded items from the store. Advice is offered by the friendly staff upon request.

6 Timbuk2
MAP F3 ■ 506 Hayes St

A brand synonymous with the city's casual backpack culture, Timbuk2 is famous for its ever-changing collection of messenger bags, backpacks, and other bags and cases which can be customized.

7 Saks Fifth Avenue
MAP P4 ■ 384 Post St

For decades, the name Saks has been synonymous with high style, and this branch of the New York mainstay is one of the best embodiments of the store's mythic élan. You'll find just about every international designer of note here.

Designer clothing at Saks Fifth Avenue

⑧ Embarcadero Centre
MAP N6 ■ Embarcadero &
Battery, Sacramento & Clay Sts

Four high-rise blocks connect
to form this sprawling shopping
center. Dominated by chain stores
such as Gap, it's probably not the
best place to find a unique souvenir.
The upper floors host restaurants
and a movie theater.

Ghirardelli Square, Fisherman's Wharf

⑨ Ghirardelli Square
MAP K1 ■ **900 North Point St**

Housing about 20 restaurants
and shops, this former chocolate
factory has become one of the
most frequented destinations in
Fisherman's Wharf (see p16). The
stores range from tourist T-shirt
shops to fine jewelry boutiques.

⑩ Westfield San Francisco Centre
MAP Q4 ■ **865 Market St**

This huge center has ten levels and
nearly 400 stores, including Nordstrom
and Bloomingdale's, a cinema, a food
court, and many fine restaurants.

TOP 10 SHOPPING AREAS

Chinatown shops, Grant Avenue

1 Grant Avenue
MAP N4
Chic shopping off Union Square,
Chinatown emporiums, and North
Beach hangouts in Upper Grant.

2 Union Street
Converted Victorian homes on this
street (see p103) house an assortment
of boutiques, bookstores, antiques
shops, restaurants, and art galleries.

3 Union Square
Traditionally the focal point of all the
best stores, including Tiffany & Co,
Armani, Cartier, Gucci, Chanel, and
more (see p89).

4 Upper Fillmore Street
MAP E2
A colorful choice of cafés, restaurants,
and boutiques, all geared to a high-
end Pacific Heights clientele.

5 Market Street
MAP Q3
A good place to find cut-rate
electronics and outlet stores, as well
as the Westfield San Francisco Centre.

6 Hayes Valley
These blocks offer galleries and stores
with an avant-garde feel (see p105).

7 Chestnut Street
MAP K1
Clothing boutiques, health-food shops,
and an old-fashioned cinema.

8 The Mission
Plenty of discount stores and funky
home furnishing shops (see pp110–11).

9 Castro Street
Fine shops, LGBTQ+ bookstores and
erotic boutiques (see p109).

10 Haight Street
The place (see p104) for secondhand
clothing, emporiums, and shoe stores.

🔟 San Francisco for Free

The Music Concourse, Golden Gate Park

1 Outdoor Summer Concerts

Sigmund Stern Recreation Grove at 19th Ave & Sloat Blvd ▪ (415) 252-6252 ▪ Open Jun–Aug: Sun ▪ www.sterngrove.org

Pines and eucalyptus create a verdant backdrop for the amphitheater where the free Stern Grove Festival concerts take place on summer Sundays. Many picnic while enjoying jazz, rock, the symphony, ballet, and opera.

2 Waterfront Ramble

The Wave Organ: MAP E1; 83 Marina Green Drive

There is a lot to enjoy for free along the waterfront. Listen to *The Wave Organ*, an acoustic wave-activated sculpture, peruse murals in the Maritime Museum *(see p51)*, stroll the Hyde Street Pier past the 1886 square-rigged ship *Balcutha*, watch sea lions at Pier 39, or bask in the misty *Fog Bridge* installation at the Exploratorium *(see p88)*.

3 Bayside View of the San Francisco Giants

MAP H3 ▪ Giants Promenade

During baseball season, it's free to watch the San Francisco Giants play at home in the Oracle Park from the Giants Promenade walkway.

4 Golden Gate Park

Opera in the Park: www.sfopera.com

This 1.5-sq-mile (4-sq-km) urban garden *(see pp24–5)* is a great place to watch tai chi classes, swing dancing, or bison roaming in their paddock. The Music Concourse hosts free concerts in summer, including the annual Opera in the Park event.

5 Fort Point National Historic Site

Situated at the foot of the Golden Gate Bridge, this fortress *(see p45)* was built in 1861 to protect the city of San Francisco from Confederate attacks that never came. Children in particular love to see the cannons being loaded, as well as the annual Civil War reenactments.

Cannon at Fort Point

6 Guided Walking Tours

(415) 557-4266

■ www.sfcityguides.org

Dozens of daily, free walking tours are led by savvy locals and historians, giving insights into Coit Tower murals, Chinatown alleys, the LGBTQ+ Castro neighborhood, Victorian architecture, the Gold Rush, and other topics.

7 City Hall

Wander through the 1915 Beaux Arts City Hall, situated in the Civic Center (see p89), which houses city government and public art. Tour guides tell of glory days and tragedies, such as the 1906 earthquake and the assassination of Mayor George Moscone in 1978 (see p43).

8 Free Museum Days

The first Tuesday of every month, museums open their doors for free, including the de Young Museum (see pp28–9) and the European-art-filled Legion of Honor (see p117). The San Francisco Museum of Craft and Design (see p51) has pay-what-you-can Wednesdays, and admission is free at the Contemporary Jewish Museum (see p50) on the first Friday of each month. Set in a stunning Beaux Arts edifice, the Asian Art Museum (see pp50–51) has free admission on the first Sunday of the month.

9 The Presidio

The Officers' Club:
www.presidioofficersclub.com

Take a ranger-led tour to experience 200 years of military history, from Spanish cannons to Civil War barracks (see pp98–9). The Officers' Club also runs free cultural events. Meander the forest trails and enjoy a picnic on the beach or in the seaview meadows.

10 Golden Gate Bridge

Whether under cloudy or sunny skies, a walk or cycle across the "international orange" Golden Gate Bridge (see pp12–13) is a pleasure. The iconic symbol of the city towers 260 ft (79 m) above churning Bay waters, and offers great views of Alcatraz Island, sailboats, freighters, and ferries.

TOP 10 BUDGET TIPS

Hardly Strictly Bluegrass festival

1 One of the largest multi-genre music festivals in the country, 3-day Hardly Strictly Bluegrass (www.hardly strictlybluegrass.com) is free to all.

2 Go San Francisco (www.smart destinations.com) Card holders get free and discounted admission to more than 25 attractions, tours, and cruises.

3 Print out the current SF Travel Coupons (www.sftravelcoupons.com) for discounted cruises, tours, attractions, shopping, and more.

4 Tix Bay Area sells half-price tickets to cultural events, both online (www. tixbayarea.org) and at the booth on Union Square.

5 Self-cater and picnic with locally sourced food from the city's world-famous farmers' markets (www.cafarmersmkts.org).

6 Happy-hour bar menus of small plates and discounted drinks are available from about 4pm to 7pm.

7 Discount coupons and special offers are available on the San Francisco Travel website (www.sftravel.com/ deals), or at the Visitor Information Center (900 Market St).

8 At some Mexican places in the Mission, delicious burritos and tacos are under $5. Chinese restaurants and food trucks also offer good value.

9 Muni has 1-, 3-, and 7-day passes offering great savings. The Clipper Pass is an all-in-one prepay pass, accepted on most transport (see pp134–5).

10 The FunCheap website (www.sf. funcheap.com) lists up-to-date free and inexpensive activities and events. Check the "today" and "weekend" calendars for what's free.

🔟 Festivals and Parades

Performer, Lunar New Year parade

dancing, as well as delicious Japanese food, making this one of the city's favorite celebrations. There is also a colorful parade.

4 Cinco de Mayo
Sat or Sun around May 5

Commemorating the defeat of the French army at Puebla, Mexico, in 1862, by General Ignacio Zaragoza, this is one of the Latin American community's biggest annual festivals, featuring parades, fireworks, music, and dancing. In addition to the Civic Center, much of the fun happens in the Mission District.

5 Carnaval
Mission District ■ Last weekend in May

Having nothing at all to do with Lent or any other traditional date, San Francisco's Carnaval is staged when the weather will most likely be at its best for the glittery event. Groups work all year long, with the help of municipal grants, to create their dazzling costumes and put together their infectiously rhythmic routines, all to a samba, rumba, or salsa beat.

1 Lunar New Year
Jan or Feb

Among the biggest Lunar New Year celebrations outside Asia, the festivities incorporate traditional displays and the parade of dragons and performers that winds through the streets of Chinatown.

2 St. Patrick's Day Parade
Sat or Sun before Mar 17

With San Francisco's large Irish population, not to mention the 25 or so Irish pubs scattered around town, the St. Patrick's Day Parade and the revelry that follows into the night is one of the city's largest celebrations. The parade journeys from 2nd and Market Streets to the Civic Center.

6 San Francisco Pride
Sat & Sun in late Jun

More than 500,000 people attend this amazing LGBTQ+ event, the largest of its kind in the US, that takes over Market Street, from the Civic Center to the Embarcadero. Expect Dykes on Bikes®, drag

3 Cherry Blossom Festival
Two weekends in Apr

Japantown *(see p103)* comes to life spectacularly when the cherry trees blossom during April. There are displays of traditional arts and crafts, *taiko* drumming, martial arts demonstrations, and

San Francisco Pride

queens in nuns' habits, LGBTQ+ marching bands, muscle men, and much more. The floats – as well as the cheering throngs – are likely to be the most colorful, vivacious things you can see any time of the year in the city.

7 Stern Grove Festival
Sun, early Jun–late Aug

A much-loved San Francisco tradition, this festival *(see p118)* showcases every kind of music in an idyllic atmosphere.

8 Independence Day
Jul 4

This festival, held from Aquatic Park to PIER 39, involves live entertainment, food stalls, and fireworks launched from several points along the Bayfront. If it's foggy, the bursts of light seem even more romantic.

The US Navy Blue Angels, Fleet Week

9 Fleet Week
Oct

A celebration of US naval forces, air shows, and a parade of ships sail into the Bay with the spectacular San Francisco skyline as a backdrop.

10 Halloween
Oct 31

Celebrated with a boisterous Castro party and parade, this is the time to wear creative costumes and let your imagination run wild.

TOP 10 FAIRS AND GATHERINGS

A Bay to Breakers participant

1 Tet Festival
Jan–Feb
A multicultural party, but mainly Vietnamese American in theme.

2 Tribal & Textile Arts Show
Feb
Arts and crafts fair at the Fort Mason Center, with pottery, jewelry, and more.

3 Bay to Breakers
Late May
Runners race in funny costumes from the Ferry Building to Ocean Beach.

4 Haight-Ashbury Street Fair
Jun
You'll see hippiedom is still alive after attending this Gathering of the Tribe.

5 North Beach Festival
Jun
The city's oldest street fair features arts and crafts and some great Italian food.

6 Fillmore Jazz Festival
Early Jul
Playing up the jazz heritage of this area, with crafts and live music.

7 Ghirardelli Square Chocolate Festival
Sep
A chocoholic's dream, with the chance to sample various nibbles.

8 Folsom Street Fair
Last Sun Sep
One of the biggest events for the LGBTQ+ community after Pride.

9 Castro Street Fair
Early Oct
A build-up to Halloween, it focuses on everyday life in the LGBTQ+ community.

10 The Portola Festival
Late Sep
Indie and electronic music festival featuring big industry names.

TOP10 Day Trips from the City

Giant redwoods in Muir Woods

1 Muir Woods

Muir Woods National Monument: (415) 388-2595; open 8am–sunset daily; adm; www.nps.gov/muwo ■ Muir Woods Shuttle: www.gomuirwoods.com

Named after the 19th-century conservationist, John Muir *(see p45)*, this 1-sq mile (2-sq km) woodland is home to some of the last-remaining first-growth redwood. Some of these giants are over 1,000 years old. As parking is limited and fills up most days, reservations are required for vehicles and the Muir Woods Shuttle.

2 Big Basin Redwoods State Park

Highway 9 is one of the most picturesque drives in the Bay Area, winding among green mountains and through little towns on the way to this park, which, although it's a relatively short drive from Silicon Valley, has a backwoods feel.

3 Los Gatos and Saratoga

Hakone Gardens: 21000 Big Basin Way, Saratoga; (408) 741-4994; open Mar–Oct: 10am–5pm Mon–Fri (from 11am Sat & Sun); Nov–Feb: 10am–4pm (from 11am Sat & Sun); adm; www.hakone.com

In the hills above Silicon Valley, and below the Santa Cruz Mountains, these historic small towns offer charming shops, restaurants, and inns *(see p128)*. One of the best things to do is to visit Hakone Gardens, a beautiful Japanese park with a tea house.

4 Monterey Peninsula

Day-trippers head to Monterey for its world-class aquarium, to shop and eat on Cannery Row (made famous by John Steinbeck), and to ramble along the shores of Point Lobos State Natural Reserve. Carmel-by-the-Sea is full of quaint cottages, art galleries, and boutique shops, as well as having a picturesque beach. Golfers make pilgrimages to visit the legendary Pebble Beach and Spanish Bay golf clubs, and to play at Bayonet Black Horse and Pacific Grove courses.

Panoramic view of a lake in Big Basin Redwoods State Park

5 Wine Country

Taking at least a day to drive up into the Napa and Sonoma valleys *(see pp36–9)* should be on everyone's San Francisco to-do list. Not only is the countryside beautiful, but also you can sample some of the best wines in the world. Dip into the restorative volcanic hot springs, and enjoy lavish spa treatments.

6 Stanford University

Located in the city of Palo Alto, with a Caltrain station right at the main gates, the palm-lined beauty of this campus *(see p126)* makes it worth a trip. The motif of sandstone and red-tile roofs has been carried forward since the Romanesque Quadrangle was built in the late 1800s. The carvings on the arches and pillars set off the elaborate mosaic that graces the facade of the Memorial Church.

7 Half Moon Bay

This charming Victorian-era town is fringed with long, sandy beaches that are perfect for strolling and surfing. Half Moon Bay State Beach is actually made up of 3 miles (5 km) of adjacent beaches, along-side which the Coastside Trail runs. The local flower farms and busy fishing port are photogenic, while fresh seafood, art galleries, and country stores add to the mix.

8 Santa Cruz

This beach resort *(see p128)* has always had a reputation for the vibrancy of its countercultural way of life. Along the beautiful coastline, the most prominent feature is the boardwalk's Giant Dipper Roller Coaster, which has been thrilling Santa Cruzers since 1924. The best swimming in the Bay Area is also here.

9 Point Reyes

Some 110 sq miles (285 sq km) of pristine natural coastline make this promontory *(see p128)* a haven for all sorts of wildlife and a thing of unforgettable, windswept beauty. You can watch whales and sea lions from Point Reyes Lighthouse.

Point Reyes Lighthouse

10 Sonoma Coast

The Tides Wharf: 835 Coast Highway One; (707) 875-3652

About an hour's scenic drive from the city are sandy beaches, rocky coves, and the fisher village of Bodega Bay. From the deck or a window table at the Tides Wharf seafood restaurant, watch harbor seals play and fishers unload their catches, then take a drive along world-famous Highway 1, stopping off at Sonoma Coast beaches.

San Francisco Area by Area

The Downtown skyline behind the "Painted Ladies" of Alamo Square

Top10 Downtown

The Downtown area is small but highly varied, including some of the city's oldest and newest landmarks. Colorful Chinatown, exuberant North Beach, posh Nob and Russian Hills, the bustling Financial District, the graceful Ferry Building, and the Beaux Arts-style architecture and culture of Civic Center; all these and more are packed into the city's heart. This is where you can ride the cable cars' most scenic routes and climb up Telegraph Hill, where Coit Tower stands as one of the city's most loved landmarks, competing with the Transamerica Pyramid not very far away.

Chinatown statue

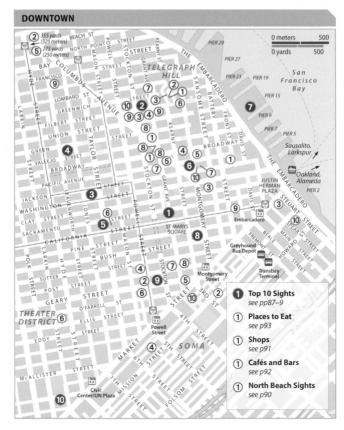

DOWNTOWN

1 Top 10 Sights
see pp87–9

1 Places to Eat
see p93

1 Shops
see p91

1 Cafés and Bars
see p92

1 North Beach Sights
see p90

1 Chinatown

Since its beginnings in the 1850s, this densely populated neighborhood (see pp22–3) has held its own powerful cultural identity despite every threat and cajolery. To walk along its cluttered, clattering streets and alleys is to be transported to another continent and into another way of life – truly a "city" within the city.

2 North Beach
MAP L4

This lively neighborhood is the original "Little Italy" of the city, and is still noted for its great Italian restaurants and cafés, mostly lined up along and near Columbus Avenue. In the 1950s, it was also a magnet for the Beat writers and poets, notably Jack Kerouac and Allen Ginsberg (see p54), who brought to the area an alternative style which it still sports today. This is a great place for nightlife, from the tawdry bawdiness of Broadway strip joints to the simple pleasures of listening to a mezzo-soprano while you sip your cappuccino.

3 Nob Hill
MAP N3

With the advent of the cable car, the highest hill in San Francisco was quickly peopled with the elaborate mansions of local magnates – in particular, the "Big Four" who built the Transcontinental Railroad (see p45) – and the name has become synonymous with wealth and power. The 1906 earthquake, however, left only one "palace" standing, now the Pacific Union Club, which still proudly dominates the center of the summit. Today, instead of private mansions, Nob Hill is home to the city's fanciest hotels and apartment buildings, as well as Grace Cathedral.

4 Russian Hill
MAP M2

Another of San Francisco's precipitous heights, one side of which is so steep you'll find no street at all, only steps. The most famous feature of this hill is the charming Lombard Street switchback – "The World's Crookedest Street" – which attests to the hill's notoriously unmanageable inclines. As with Nob Hill, with the cable car's advent, Russian Hill was claimed by the wealthy, and it maintains a lofty position in San Francisco society to this day. It supposedly took its name from the burial place of Russian fur traders, who were among the first Europeans to ply their trade at this port in the early 1800s.

5 Grace Cathedral

MAP N3 ▪ 1100 California St ▪ (415) 749-6300 ▪ Open from 8am daily (from 7am Thu), closing hours vary ▪ www.gracecathedral.org

Inspired by French Gothic architecture, with dazzling stained-glass windows and towers topping 170 ft (50 m), this Episcopal cathedral is a photogenic landmark on Nob Hill.

Stained glass at Grace Cathedral

THE MAKING OF A CITY

Europeans first landed at the Bay in 1769, and for years it was little more than a Mission village. Later, the Bay became Mexican in 1821. Gold was found in 1848 and people from all over the world came to the area (below) to try their luck. At the same time, the US took possession of the West Coast. The Transcontinental Railroad helped to establish its financial base.

6 Jackson Square
MAP M5

This neighborhood by the Transamerica Pyramid *(see p48)* contains some of the city's oldest buildings. In the 19th century it was notorious for its squalor, and was nicknamed the "Barbary Coast," but brothels and drinking establishments have given way to offices and antiques shops. The blocks around Jackson Street and Hotaling Place feature many original facades.

Jackson Square plaque

7 Exploratorium
MAP L6 ■ Pier 15, Embarcadero ■ (415) 528-4360 ■ Museum: open 10am–5pm Tue–Sun ■ Adm ■ www. exploratorium.edu

One of the world's first hands-on science museums, the Exploratorium *(see p65)* now stands in a spectacular location on Pier 15. There are close to 600 exhibits that are spread among themed indoor galleries and a large outside space. There are also educational programs, a theater, an interactive gift shop, a Bay Observatory, an outdoor plaza, and cafés.

8 Financial District
MAP M5

Montgomery Street, now the heart of the Financial District, was once lined with small shops where miners came to weigh their gold dust. It marks roughly the old shoreline of shallow Yerba Buena Cove, which was filled in during the Gold Rush to create more land. Today it is lined with banking "temples" of the early 20th century and modern fabrications of glass and steel. At the end of Market Street stands the Ferry Building, which handled 100,000 commuters per day before the city's bridges were constructed, and is now a bustling meeting spot with cafés and artisan food shops. Its tower is inspired by the Moorish belfry of Seville's cathedral in Spain.

Skyscrapers of the Financial District

A WALK AROUND NORTH BEACH

Art on display in Union Square

9 Union Square
MAP P4

This important square, which gets its name from the pro-Union rallies held here in the early 1860s, has a $25-million upgraded look that includes performance spaces and grassy terraces. It is now the center for high-end shopping (see p77). With the Financial District on one side and the Theater District on the other, it is most picturesque along Powell Street, where the cable cars pass in front of the historic Westin St. Francis hotel (see p143). Its central column commemorates Admiral Dewey's victory at Manila Bay during the Spanish American War of 1898.

10 Civic Center
MAP R1

The city's elaborate Beaux Arts administrative center includes the grand City Hall, the War Memorial Opera House, the Louise M. Davies Symphony Hall (see p66), the Herbst Theater, the State Building and the new Main Library. The old Main Library was re-inaugurated as the stellar Asian Art Museum (see p50) in 2003. The much grittier Tenderloin district is directly to the north, and the charming Hayes Valley (see p105) is just southwest.

MORNING

Start at the top of North Beach, on **Telegraph Hill** (see p90), admire the famous views, and visit **Coit Tower** (see p48), making sure to take in the murals. Next, walk down to **Filbert Street Steps** (see p90) and go right a couple of blocks until you get to lovely **Washington Square** (see p90), where, at the Catholic **Saints Peter and Paul Church** (see p90), Marilyn Monroe and local baseball great Joe DiMaggio had their wedding pictures taken. Continue on and pay a visit to **Mario's Bohemian Cigar Store Cafe** (566 Columbus Ave; (415) 362-0536), where you can indulge in a bit of people-watching. Or, just behind on Stockton Street, head to **Tony's Pizza Napoletana** (1570 Stockton St; (415) 835-9888), for its award-winning pizza.

AFTERNOON

After lunch, take a left on Green Street and go over one block to **Upper Grant** (see p90), with its funky shops and bars, a regular hangout since the 1950s. Turn right on to Vallejo Street, where a visit to the famous **Caffè Trieste** (see p92) for a coffee and the artistic atmosphere is a must. Continue to **Specs'** (12 William Saroyan Pl; www.specsbarsf.com), an exuberant bar filled with Beat memorabilia. Finally, just across Columbus is the immortal **City Lights Bookstore** (see p90), where you can browse the Beat poetry written by owner Lawrence Ferlinghetti and friends.

See map on p86

North Beach Sights

A colorful mural at Coit Tower

1 Coit Tower
MAP L5

The frescoes in this tower (see p48) were painted by local artists in 1934, to provide jobs during the Depression. The murals give socio-political commentary and details of life in California at the time.

2 North Beach Views
The panoramic views from both the hill and the top of the Coit Tower are justly celebrated. The wide arc sweeping from the East Bay and the Bay Bridge to Alcatraz and the Golden Gate Bridge is breathtaking.

3 Telegraph Hill
MAP L5

Named after the semaphore installed on its crest in 1850. The hill's eastern side was dynamited to provide rocks for landfill. Steps descend its slopes, lined with gardens. At its summit is Coit Tower.

4 Broadway
MAP M5

Made famous in the 1960s for its various adult entertainments. The offerings haven't changed much, though today many venues are now more mainstream.

5 City Lights Bookstore
MAP M4 ■ 261 Columbus Ave ■ (415) 362-8193

The Beat poet Lawrence Ferlinghetti founded City Lights in 1953. It's a great place to leaf through a few volumes of poetry or the latest free papers to find out what's on.

6 Filbert Street Steps
MAP L5

The flowery descent down these steps provides great Bay views.

7 Upper Grant
MAP L4

Saloons, cafés, and bluesy music haunts give this northerly section of Grant Avenue a very alternative feel.

8 Caffè Trieste
If you're in the neighborhood on a Saturday afternoon, don't miss the spirited opera that takes place here (see p92). It is one of the longest-running musical shows in the city.

9 Washington Square
MAP L4

This pretty park is lined with Italian bakeries, restaurants, and bars. Don't be surprised to see practitioners of tai chi doing their thing on the lawn every morning.

10 Saints Peter and Paul Church
MAP L4 ■ 666 Filbert St ■ Open daily

Neo-Gothic in conception, with an Italianesque facade, this church (see p46) is also called the Italian Cathedral and the Fisherman's Church, since many Italians who originally lived in the neighborhood made their living by fishing.

Saints Peter and Paul Church

Shops

Interior of Molinari Delicatessen

1 Molinari Delicatessen
MAP G2 ■ 373 Columbus Ave
■ www.themolinarideli.com

Part of the neighborhood's Italian-American heritage, Molinari's has been in business since 1896. Stop by for excellent sandwiches, fresh ravioli, whole salami, Italian soft drinks, and other delights.

2 Lola of North Beach
MAP K2 ■ 900 North Point St
■ (415) 567-7760

A charming souvenir store, Lola of North Beach features a massive collection of trinkets and cards that are uniquely San Franciscan. Ever-popular items include a selection of enamel pins and vibrant stickers.

3 Goorin Bros.
MAP L4 ■ 1612 Stockton St
■ (415) 402-0454

One of the city's finest hat shops prides itself on offering excellent service. Most of the custom hats are handmade in the US.

4 Little Vine
MAP P4 ■ 1541 Grant Ave
■ (415) 738-2221

Grab one of the sandwich specials sold here while browsing this quaint, European-inspired shop, filled with independently produced wines, artisan cheeses, pickles, and locally sourced honey.

5 Serge Sorokko Gallery
MAP P4 ■ 55 Geary St
■ (415) 421-7770

If you're in the market for a piece by one of the modern masters, this is an excellent place to browse important prints and other works by Picasso, Matisse, Miró, Chagall, and other 20th-century greats, such as Tapiès, Bacon, Twombly, and Warhol.

6 Christopher-Clark Fine Art
MAP P4 ■ 377 Geary St
■ (415) 397-7781

A gallery for modern European and American masters. A good stock of Bay Area artists, too.

7 Shreve & Co
MAP P4 ■ 150 Post St
■ (415) 421-2600

A San Francisco original and one of the most elegant jewelers to be found in the city. In addition to gems set in wonderful ways, you'll also find fine timepieces, Limoges porcelain, and Lalique crystal.

8 The North Face
MAP P4 ■ 180 Post St
■ (415) 433-3223

Originating in San Francisco, you'll find everything for the outdoor adventurer at this popular chain.

9 Macchiarini Creative Design
MAP G2 ■ 1544 Grant Ave
■ (415) 982-2229

The oldest ongoing arts design house, production studio, and gallery in the US, hand-crafting individually made sculptures and jewelry.

10 William Stout Architectural Books
MAP M4 ■ 804 Montgomery St
■ (415) 391-6757

A landmark for design buffs all over the world, this small shop is divided into two spaces, with newer books on display upstairs.

See map on p86

Cafés and Bars

Visitors enjoying coffee in the outdoor seating area at Caffè Trieste

1 Caffè Trieste
MAP M4 ■ 609 Vallejo St
■ (415) 982-2605

One of the most popular cafés
(see p74) in the city, rich with an
arty sense of nonchalance.

2 ENO Wine Bar
MAP P3 ■ 320 Geary St ■ (415)
678-5321 ■ www.enowinerooms.com

A laid-back bar, ENO offers a range
of wines, cheeses, and chocolates.

3 Punch Line Comedy Club
MAP M5 ■ 444 Battery St ■ (415)
397-7573 ■ www.punchlinecomedy
club.com

Performances by talented local and
national comedians will leave you in
splits at this venue *(see p69)*.

4 Blue Bottle Café
MAP Q4 ■ 66 Mint St ■ (510)
653-3394

A cool, modern space *(see p74)* known
for its hip crowd, and for turning out
some of the city's best coffee.

5 The Cheese School
MAP F1 ■ 2535 3rd St
■ www.thecheeseschool.com

Learn how to make different cheeses
and create your own charcuterie
plate here. You can also try superb
cheese boards and other snacks.

6 The Tonga Room and Hurricane Bar
MAP N3 ■ Fairmont Hotel, 950
Mason St ■ (415) 772-5278 ■ Closed
Mon & Tue ■ www.tongaroom.com

A Tiki-style lounge *(see p68)* offering
tropical tunes and cocktails.

7 The Hidden Vine
MAP M5 ■ 408 Merchant St
■ (415) 674-3567 ■ www.thehidden
vine.com

Set at the base of the Transamerica
Pyramid, this cozy wine bar *(see
p69)* features a bocce court.

8 Vesuvio Café
MAP M4 ■ 255 Columbus Ave
■ (415) 362-3370

This North Beach mainstay *(see p75)*
serves potent drinks and is close to
the City Lights Bookstore *(see p90)*.

9 Bimbo's 365 Club
MAP K3 ■ 1025 Columbus Ave
■ (415) 474-0365 ■ www.bimbos
365club.com

Around since 1931, Bimbo's *(see
p69)* features live music, comedy,
and iconic holiday parties.

10 Press Club
MAP P4 ■ 20 Yerba Buena
Lane at Market ■ (415) 744-5000

This popular and ultramodern lounge
offers a wide selection of wines.

Places to Eat

PRICE CATEGORIES
For a three-course meal for one with half a bottle of wine (or equivalent meal), taxes, and extra charges.

$ under $40   **$$** $40–$80   **$$$** over $80

1 Kokkari Estiatorio
MAP M6 ■ 200 Jackson St ■ (415) 981-0983 ■ $$$

The Greek cuisine here is a delectable revelation of flavors. The lamb shank and grilled octopus are not to be missed.

2 Mourad
MAP G3 ■ 140 New Montgomery St ■ (415) 660-2500 ■ $$$

Dine on Moroccan food, while sitting in a booth, in a historic building (see p72).

3 One Market
MAP N6 ■ 1 Market St at Steuart ■ (415) 777-5577 ■ Closed Sun ■ $$

The views of the Bay's lights from here (see p75) are spectacular at night. Enjoy the farm-fresh food.

4 Sears Fine Food
MAP P4 ■ 439 Powell St ■ (415) 986-0700/1160 ■ $

This 1950s retro coffee shop (see p75) is famous for its break-fasts, and is always a reliable choice for a quick fill-up.

Entrance to Sears Fine Food

5 Quince
MAP M5 ■ 470 Pacific Ave ■ (415) 775-8500 ■ Closed L ■ $$$

The tasting menu made with local ingredients, has earned rave reviews for this Michelin-starred restaurant (see p72).

Grapefruit mousse, Quince

6 Lers Ros Thai
MAP K2 ■ 730 Larkin St ■ (415) 931-6917 ■ $

This restaurant (see p73) lives up to it's name – in Sanskrit, 'lers' translates as 'excellent' and 'ros' means 'taste'.

7 Trestle
MAP M5 ■ 531 Jackson St ■ (415) 772-0922 ■ $

A cozy little bistro with a welcoming vibe, Trestle offers an elegant three-course prix fixe menu.

8 Sotto Mare
MAP L4 ■ 552 Green St ■ (415) 398-3181 ■ $$

Housed in a 19th-century building on a busy Little Italy street, Sotto Mare serves Italian seafood dishes. Don't miss the crab *cioppino*.

9 Tadich Grill
MAP N5 ■ 240 California St ■ (415) 391-1849 ■ $$

Beginning as a coffee stand in 1849, today this traditional restaurant serves classics such as clam chowder. Brusque staff add some fun to the atmosphere. No reservations required.

10 Yank Sing
MAP H2 ■ 101 Spear St ■ (415) 781-1111 ■ $$

Head to the busy Rincon Center in SoMA for excellent Chinese cuisine. Yank Sing is famous for its signature Shanghai dumplings, with over 60 varieties on offer.

See map on p86 ←

TOP 10 The North Shoreline

San Francisco began to grow along the North Shoreline when the Spanish set up a military outpost at the Presidio in 1776. Today the shoreline is a showcase of both historical and modern attractions. The Palace of Fine Arts recalls the 1915 Panama-Pacific International Exposition; the vintage homes of the Marina District have stellar Bay views; ships depart from Pier 41 for Bay cruises; and tourists crowd the stores and seafood restaurants of Fisherman's Wharf. Walk all the way from the Golden Gate Bridge to the Embarcadero to get a sense of the many eras of the "Paris of the West."

Embarcadero street sign

1 Angel and Treasure Islands

Ferries from San Francisco Ferry Building

A trip out to Angel Island, now a state park, can mean a day of picnicking, biking, hiking, kayaking, or swimming. But in the early 1900s it was the "Ellis Island of the West," where would-be immigrants, mostly Chinese, could be detained for months on end. During World War II, it served as a prisoner of war camp and then later as a missile base. Treasure Island was built in 1939 for the Golden Gate International Exposition and served as a US Navy base during World War II. It is now once again owned by the city of San Francisco and is one of its suburbs.

2 Golden Gate Bridge

This renowned masterpiece of engineering *(see pp12–13)* sets off the entrance to San Francisco Bay in a spectacular way. It never fails to awe both first-timers and old-timers alike. Walking or cycling across its length is an unforgettable experience.

3 Alcatraz

America's "Devil's Island" *(see pp18–21)* didn't operate as a

---

THE NORTH SHORELINE

San Francisco Bay

GOLDEN GATE BRIDGE FWY

MARINE DRIVE

MARINE DRIVE

OLD MASON STREET

PRESIDIO PKWY

LINCOLN

SHERIDAN AVE

MARINA BLVD

BRODERICK STREET

BAKER STREET

RICHARDSON AVENUE

DIVISADERO ST

SCOTT STREET

LOMBA

- **1** **Top 10 Sights**
  see pp96–9
- ① **Places to Eat**
  see p101
- ① **Fisherman's Wharf Area Shops**
  see p100

Previous pages Alcatraz Island and the San Francisco skyline

Alcatraz as seen from the prison gardens

prison for a particularly long time, but the cell blocks and control room still manage to evoke a chill.

4 Fisherman's Wharf

Although now largely tourist-oriented, there are still traditional maritime sights to see, aromas to savor, and salt air to breathe along these piers *(see pp16–17)*. Pier 39 is a highlight, with its various amusements, shops, and restaurants.

5 The Embarcadero
MAP G1

Skirted with palm trees, the Embarcadero runs from the North

Shoreline down to the coast of Downtown, from Pier 45 to the San Francisco Giants' AT&T Park. It is lined with attractions and departure points for cruise ships. The Alcatraz Landing is at Pier 33 and Hornblower Cruises leaves from Pier 3. Scenic views can be enjoyed at the pedestrianized piers 7 and 14. On the south waterfront, you'll find the 60-ft- (18-m-) tall *Cupid's Span*. It is a simple sculpture of the god's bow and arrow, which is half buried in the ground. It perfectly represents the city's romantic reputation. Piers north of the Ferry Building have odd numbers, while those to the south have even numbers.

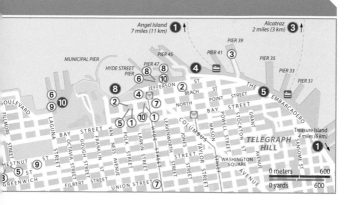

The Golden Gate Bridge viewed from Crissy Field

6 Crissy Field
MAP D1

Originally marshland and dunes, the field was filled in before the 1915 Panama-Pacific Exposition and paved over for use as an airfield by the army from 1919 to 1936. With the establishment of the Presidio as a national park under the supervision of the city, a massive restoration project has returned part of Crissy Field to wetlands and the rest to lawns, pathways, and picnic areas. The city's over 4 million-sq ft (370,000-sq m) "Front Yard" is one of the prime viewing sites for the Fourth of July fireworks. Extending over 4-miles (7-km), the Golden Gate Promenade is a paved pathway that runs through this district from Aquatic Park to Fort Point.

7 Fort Point
MAP C1

Crashing waves, passing ships, and windsurfers, along with a Civil War-era fort loaded with cannons, guns, and other military artifacts, make for spectacular photos here beneath the Golden Gate Bridge (see p12). You can fish along the seawall and take self-guided or ranger-led tours to learn about the building of the bridge. At the foot of the cliffs on the western side of the fort is a small beach loved by nude sun worshippers.

8 Aquatic Park
MAP F1 ■ Visitor Center: 499 Jefferson St; (415) 447-5000; open 9:30am–5pm Sun–Fri

Within the sheltering arm of a curved fishing pier is the warmest, safest Bayside beach. Sometimes signs advise against swimming – look out before taking a dip in the cold water. Joggers and bikers love the paved trail. The cable car turnaround is steps away at Beach and Hyde Streets. In the park you will find a Visitor Center and the Maritime Museum (see p50).

9 The Presidio
MAP D2

This wooded corner of the city has stunning views over the Golden Gate. From 1776 until 1994, it was

Disney museum exhibit, The Presidio

EARTHQUAKE! THE LANDFILL PROBLEM

Most of the Marina area, as well as the majority of the Financial District, was built on landfill. As time has proven, this was not such a good idea in a seismically active zone. When the Loma Prieta earthquake struck at 5:04pm on October 17, 1989, all such landfills liquefied, gas mains fractured, and several Marina homes slid off their foundations. Buildings that withstand best are those built on bedrock, which includes most of the inland areas of the city.

occupied by first the Spanish, then the Mexican, and finally, the US armies. It is now a major part of the Golden Gate National Recreational Area. It is full of nature trails, streams, forests, drives, and historic structures. Also here is the Walt Disney Family Museum, which gives insight into Walt Disney's life through photographs, animation, and a range of interactive exhibits.

The waterfront by Fort Mason Center

⑩ Fort Mason Center
MAP F1

Since 1976 some of the buildings at this Civil War-era military base have been devoted to cultural programs. Some 50 cultural organizations now call it home. Among the most prominent are the Museo Italo Americano (see p53), the Long Now Foundation, the Children's Art Center and the Magic Theater (see p67). One of the city's finest vegetarian restaurant, Greens, is also here, offering great views of the Bay (see p72).

A BIKE RIDE THROUGH THE PRESIDIO

Beginning at the Visitor Information Center, where you can pick up an excellent map, first explore the Main Post. Here you can ride around the Parade Ground and see the earliest surviving buildings of the Presidio, dating from the 1860s, as well as 18th-century Spanish adobe wall fragments in the former Officers' Club.

Exit the area on Sheridan Avenue, which takes you past the Spanish Colonial Revival-style Golden Gate Club, and turn left onto Lincoln Boulevard, which winds its way around the National Military Cemetery. Turn right on McDowell Avenue; on the left you will see the Colonial Revival Cavalry Barracks.

Now go past the five brick Stables, off to both the left and the right, and stop at the quirky Pet Cemetery on the left, where guard dogs are buried as well as many family pets. Next, head under Highway 101 to encounter Stilwell Hall, built in 1921 as enlisted barracks and a mess hall for the airmen. Turn left to take in the metal Aerodrome Hangars from the same era, then proceed on down to Crissy Field to admire the views.

Double back at this point to take the next left down toward the Bay itself and join the Golden Gate Promenade all the way out to Fort Point. As long as the fog is not too bad, this is the perfect spot to experience the awe-inspiring Golden Gate Bridge (see pp12–13) and the crashing waves of the mighty Pacific.

See map on pp96–7 ←

Fisherman's Wharf Area Shops

1 Ghirardelli Chocolate

MAP K2 ■ Ghirardelli Square, 900 North Point St ■ (415) 447-2846

Stop by for a free sample and then stock up on your mouthwatering favorites. Take home some chocolate cable cars.

Ghirardelli Chocolate

2 Gigi + Rose

MAP K2 ■ Ghirardelli Square, 900 North Point St ■ (415) 765-9060

Quirky gifts, accessories, and children's outfits, many of which are designed by the owners, are for sale.

3 Alcatraz Gift Shop

MAP J4 ■ 2nd level, Pier 39 ■ (415) 249-4666

Souvenirs of the Rock, from tin cups to prisoner outfits are for sale here. Photos and history books can be found at the Alcatraz Book Store on Pier 41.

4 Real Old Paper

MAP F1 ■ 777 Beach St ■ www.realoldpaper.com

Discover a beautiful selection of authentic vintage posters from the US and elsewhere here.

5 Jackson & Polk

MAP K2 ■ Ghirardelli Square, 900 North Point St ■ (415) 345-9708

A little bit of everything is on offer in this boutique of books and treasures, which prides itself on offering a wide selection of San Francisco-based brands.

6 V Boutique

MAP F1 ■ 435 Jefferson St ■ (415) 757-0043

This boutique selling stylish clothing for women is part of VenturaVie, a non-profit funding local charity organizations and supporting local causes.

7 Patagonia

MAP J4 ■ 770 North Point St ■ (415) 771-2050

The San Francisco store of this quintessentially Californian company sells classic fleeces and outdoor wear. One per cent of annual sales is donated to environmental charities.

8 Alioto-Lazio Fish Co

MAP F1 ■ 440 Jefferson St ■ (415) 673-5868

One of the last family-owned and operated fishing companies in San Francisco, Alioto-Lazio connects you to San Francisco's briny and delicious culinary heritage.

9 Readers Bookstore

MAP F1 ■ Fort Mason Center, 2 Marina Blvd ■ (415) 771-1076

Great secondhand books, records, and CDs, with all the proceeds supporting programs in San Francisco's libraries. You won't find better prices anywhere else.

10 Frank's Fisherman Supply

MAP E1 ■ 366 Jefferson St ■ (415) 775-1165

Frank's has been selling ship models, rare navigation devices, paintings, marine antiques, and various historic ship paraphernalia since 1946.

Merchandise at Jackson & Polk

Places to Eat

PRICE CATEGORIES

For a three-course meal for one with half a bottle of wine (or equivalent meal), taxes, and extra charges.

$ under $40 $$ $40–$80 $$$ over $80

1 Gary Danko

MAP K2 ■ 800 North Point St at Hyde ■ (415) 749-2060 ■ $$$

The French American menu served here allows you to create your own fixed-price selection. If you don't have a reservation (which are taken up to two months in advance), head for the bar, where you can order anything on the menu.

Interior of Gary Danko restaurant

2 The Codmother

MAP J4 ■ 496 Beach St ■ (415) 606-9349 ■ Closed D ■ $

This food truck serves outstanding fish tacos, fish and chips, and assorted chip-shop desserts, such as fried Oreos.

3 Isa

MAP E2 ■ 3324 Steiner St between Chestnut & Lombard ■ (415) 567-9588 ■ Closed L ■ $$

At this tiny Marina restaurant, the concept is Nouvelle French tapas, with small plates such as honey-spiced calamari and lobster broth sprinkled with tarragon.

4 A16

MAP E1 ■ 2355 Chestnut St ■ (415) 771-2216 ■ $$

A traditional southern Italian dining experience that's worth getting dressed up for *(see p72)*.

Diners outside the popular Tacolicious

5 Tacolicious

MAP K4 ■ 2250 Chestnut St ■ (415) 649-6077 ■ $

A multitude of taco choices are served at this popular joint. Enjoy the free chips and salsa while you wait.

6 Greens

MAP F1 ■ Fort Mason Center, Buchanan St, Building A ■ (415) 771-6222 ■ $$

Since 1979, the inventive vegetarian dishes and Bayside panoramas here *(see p72)* have delighted patrons.

7 Frascati

MAP L2 ■ 1901 Hyde St ■ (415) 928-1406 ■ $$

In a cozy atmosphere, Frascati *(see p73)* offers Mediterranean cuisine with a Californian twist.

8 Scoma's

MAP J2 ■ 1965 Al Scoma Way ■ (415) 771-4383 ■ $$

A Fisherman's Wharf seafood tradition since 1965, Scoma's *(see p72)* offers cracked crab roasted in garlic.

9 Zushi Puzzle

MAP F2 ■ 1910 Lombard St ■ (415) 931-9319 ■ Closed L ■ $$

This spot serves some of the city's best sushi.

10 The Buena Vista Café

MAP K2 ■ 2765 Hyde St ■ (415) 474-5044 ■ $

This café *(see p74)* claims to have invented Irish coffee. The menu features classic American dishes.

See map on pp96–7

ᴛᴏᴘ10 Central Neighborhoods

As is the case with most parts of San Francisco, diversity is the keynote here. This area encompasses the oldest money and the highest society of the founding families of the city, as well as some of its poorest citizens. Here you can trace the evolution of San Francisco, from the sophisticated old streets of Pacific Heights and Presidio Heights, via the hippie-era Flower Power of Haight-Ashbury to the newly redeveloped neighborhoods such as Hayes Valley, buzzing with boutiques and trendy places to eat and drink.

Haight Street sign

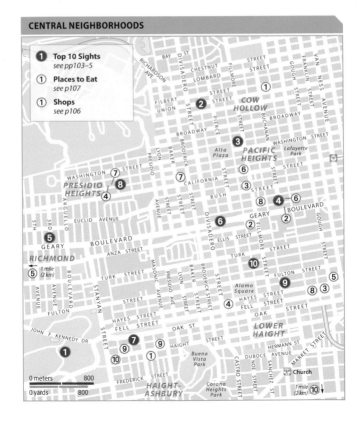

CENTRAL NEIGHBORHOODS

- **1** Top 10 Sights
  see pp103–5
- **①** Places to Eat
  see p107
- **①** Shops
  see p106

Grand facades of Victorian houses in Pacific Heights

1 Golden Gate Park
One of the largest public parks in the world *(see pp24–5)* complete with cultural attractions including the California Academy of Sciences and the de Young Museum.

2 Union Street
MAP E2

A neighborhood shopping artery loaded with tradition, Union Street *(see p77)* is noted for its sidewalk cafés, bookstores, and designer boutiques, housed in converted Victorian charmers. The street is at the heart of the Cow Hollow neighborhood, whose name recalls its previous life as a dairy pasture.

3 Pacific Heights
MAP E2

A grander, more exclusive residential area is hard to imagine. Commanding as it does heights of up to 300 ft (100 m) over-looking the magnificent Bay, everything about it proclaims power and wealth. The blocks between Alta Plaza and Lafayette parks are the very heart of the area, but the grandeur extends from Gough to Divisadero Street and beyond. On a sunny day, there's noth-ing more exhilarating

than scaling its hills and taking in the perfectly manicured streets, the views, and the palatial dwellings. The Spreckels Mansion, a limestone palace in the Beaux Arts tradition, on Washington and Octavia Streets, is the brightest gem of the lot, now owned by the novelist Danielle Steel.

4 Japantown
MAP F3

This neighborhood has been the focus of the Japanese community since the early 20th century. The Japan Center was built as part of an ambitious 1960s plan to revitalize the Fillmore District. Blocks of aging Victorian buildings were demolished and replaced by the Geary Expressway and this Japanese-style shopping complex with a five-tiered, 75-ft (22-m) Peace Pagoda at its heart. *Taiko* drummers perform here during the Cherry Blossom Festival each April *(see p80)*. The extensive malls are lined with authentic Japanese shops and restaurants, plus an eight-screen cinema, and the Kabuki Springs and Spa. More shops and restaurants can be found along the outdoor mall across Post Street.

Japantown Peace Pagoda

FLOWER POWER

In 1967, San Francisco witnessed the Summer of Love *(see p43)*, including a 75,000-strong Human Be-In at Golden Gate Park. People were drawn here – many with flowers in their hair – by the acid-driven melodies of Jefferson Airplane, Janis Joplin, Jimi Hendrix, and The Doors. Love was free, concerts were free, drugs were free, even food and healthcare were free. Soon, however, public alarm, and too many bad acid trips, caused the bubble to burst. In 2017, a variety of special events and exhibitions were held throughout the city to celebrate the 50th anniversary of the Summer of Love.

Streetcar lines at Geary Boulevard

 The Richmond District
MAP C3

This flat district of row houses begins at Masonic Street, sandwiched between Golden Gate Park and California Street. It ultimately extends all the way to the Pacific Ocean, being more and more prone to stay fog-bound the farther west you go. The district is very multicultural and generally middle class. Over the decades, it has been settled by Russians, East European Jews, and latterly Chinese Americans and another wave of Russians.

Holy Virgin Cathedral, Richmond District

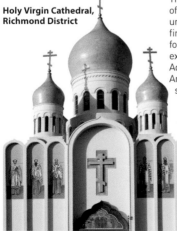

 Geary Boulevard
MAP F3

One of the city's main traffic arteries, sweeping from Van Ness all the way out to Cliff House, Geary Boulevard is a typically unprepossessing and functional urban thoroughfare. It begins its journey at Market Street, sweeps past Union Square, and then forms the heart of the Theater District, before venturing into the notorious Tenderloin, home to seedy clubs. After it crosses Van Ness, it zips past Japantown and the funky Fillmore District. Soon you're in the Richmond District and before you know it, there's the Pacific Ocean.

 Haight-Ashbury
MAP D4

This anarchic quarter is one of the most scintillating and unconventional in the city, resting firmly on its laurels as ground zero for the worldwide Flower Power explosion of the 1960s *(see p43)*. Admire the beautiful old Queen Anne-style houses, a few of them still painted in the psychedelic pigments of the hippie era, as well as the unique shops and the venerable Haight-Ashbury Free Clinic. The Lower Haight is noted for its edgy clubs and bars.

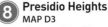 **Presidio Heights**
MAP D3

Originally part of the "Great Sand Waste" to the west, this neighborhood is now one of the most elite of all. The zone centers on Sacramento Street as its discreet shopping area. It's worth a stroll, primarily for the architecture. Of interest are the Swedenborgian Church at 2107 Lyon Street, the Roos House at 3500 Jackson Street, and Temple Emanu-El at 2 Lake Street.

9 Hayes Valley
MAP F4

This small area has seen a massive change over the past few decades. Once a run-down neighborhood, Hayes Valley is now synonymous with great boutique shopping and popular cafés. The dismantling of an unsightly freeway overpass following the 1989 earthquake helped turn the tide, and the welcome result is a chic area that hasn't lost its edge. Hayes Valley festivals take place in midsummer, when the area's streets are thronged with revelers.

Alamo Square, Western Addition

10 Western Addition
MAP E3

This area, too, was once sandy waste, but after World War II the district became populated by Southern African Americans who traveled west looking for work. For a short time it was famous for jazz and blues clubs, as embodied by John Lee Hooker and his Boom Boom Room, until his death in 2001. Today, the area is best known for getting a snapshot of local life, plus seeing the architecturally odd Cathedral of St. Mary of the Assumption *(see p46)* and photo-genic Alamo Square *(see p49)*.

A TOUR OF HAIGHT-ASHBURY

 MORNING

Begin at **Alamo Square** *(see p49)*, with the Westerfeld House at 1198 Fulton at Scott, former residence of Ken Kesey, the writer and visionary who arguably got the whole 1960s movement going. Walk up Scott, turn right on Page and go to No. 1090, where the rock band Big Brother and the Holding Company got their start. A block and a half farther on, go right on Lyon to No. 122, where Janis Joplin *(see p55)* lived for most of 1967.

Continue on to the **Panhandle** *(Stanyan St & Fell St)*, an extension of Golden Gate Park, where in June 1967 the Jimi Hendrix Experience gave a free concert. Now turn left on Central and head up to steep **Buena Vista Park** *(Buena Vista & Haight St)*, site of public Love-Ins in the 1960s and 1970s. Turn right on Haight and check out **Jammin On Haight** *(1400 Haight St at Masonic)*, which is one of the fanciest indie shops.

Continue on to the Haight-Ashbury intersection and walk along Haight to Clayton; at No. 558 is the much-loved **Haight-Ashbury Free Clinic**, still imbued with the spirit of the 1960s. Later, stop in for a snack at **Blue Front Café** *(see p107)*.

Refreshed, walk toward Golden Gate Park, then turn right on Stanyan all the way to Fulton. At 2400 Fulton stands the former **Jefferson Airplane Mansion**, which used to be painted black. Finally, head into **Golden Gate Park** *(see pp24–5)* and make your way to the drum circles on Hippie Hill to groove to the tribal beats.

See map on p102 ←

Shops

Colorful facade of The Love of Ganesha

1 The Love of Ganesha
MAP E4 ■ 1573 Haight St
■ (415) 863-0999

More than just a clothing store, this unique boutique features a wide selection of crystals, stones, and other natural knickknacks that you can't find anywhere else in the city.

2 Daiso Japan
MAP F3 ■ 22 Peace Plaza
■ (415) 359-9397

Discount store selling Japanese household items, snacks, and other fun imports.

3 Dark Garden
MAP F4 ■ 321 Linden St
■ (415) 431-7684

Popular shop for women's couture and locally made, custom, and ready-to-wear corsets, dresses, and wedding gowns. Famous clients include Christina Aguilera and Dita Von Teese.

4 Dottie Doolittle
MAP D3 ■ 3680 Sacramento St
■ (415) 563-3244

A long-established mainstay, this high-end clothier carries fashionable American and European labels for babies and kids up to the age of 12.

5 Past Perfect
MAP B3 ■ 6101 Geary Blvd
■ (415) 929-2288

There is tons to choose from at this huge, fairly priced vintage store. Plan to spend a while perusing their unique furniture, lighting, and art – there is something for everyone here. The staff are friendly, too.

6 Forest Books
MAP F3 ■ 1748 Buchanan St
■ (415) 563-8302

Specializing in second-hand, rare, and collectible books, this inviting, family-run bookshop sells excellent titles across fiction, philosophy, Eastern religions, and spirituality.

7 Sue Fisher King
MAP F2 ■ 3067 Sacramento St
■ (415) 922-7276

In 1978, Sue Fisher King opened her shop of trinkets and treasures for the home, fine jewelry, and divinely scented bath products. Today, it's still considered one of the city's must-visits.

8 Isotope – The Comic Book Lounge
MAP F4 ■ 326 Fell St ■ (415) 621-6543

With plenty of space for customers to browse and sit, Isotope offers comics, graphic novels, and handmade zines. Local artists are often invited for talks and book signings, and the owner is happy to personally help shoppers.

9 Relic Vintage
MAP E4 ■ 1475 Haight St
■ (415) 255-7460

The city's most carefully curated vintage clothing, from suits to swing coats, can be found at this welcoming Haight Street shop. Owner Oran Scott is always dressed to the nines.

10 Amoeba Music
MAP D4 ■ 1855 Haight St
■ (415) 831-1200

Besides thousands of LPs, tapes, and CDs, there's also a huge selection of DVDs and posters at this record store *(see p76)*, which is part of a chain, and prides itself on being the world's largest independent music store.

Places to Eat

PRICE CATEGORIES
For a three-course meal for one with half
a bottle of wine (or equivalent meal),
taxes, and extra charges.

$ under $40 $$ $40–$80 $$$ over $80

1 Perry's
MAP F2 ■ 1944 Union St
■ (415) 922-9022 ■ $

A San Francisco institution, noted for
its burgers and other all-American
favorites, including meatloaf, prime
rib, and fried chicken.

2 State Bird Provisions
MAP F3 ■ 1529 Fillmore St
■ (415) 795-1272 ■ $$$

A trendy Michelin-starred restaurant
serving small plates of French and
American food. Choose most of your
food from a cart or tray of dishes
brought out by the waiting staff.

3 SPQR
MAP E3 ■ 1911 Fillmore St
■ (415) 771-7779 ■ $$$

Reservations are required at this
no-frills, rustic Roman-inspired
restaurant with mouthwatering
antipasti and superior service.

4 Nopa
MAP E4 ■ 560 Divisadero St
■ (415) 864-8643 ■ Closed L ■ $$

Considered one of the best
restaurants in the city, Nopa
has a seasonally changing menu.

Interior of Nopa

German chocolate cake at Absinthe

5 Absinthe
MAP F4 ■ 398 Hayes St
■ (415) 551-1590 ■ $$

This Parisian-style bistro *(see p75)*
serves specials such as the
extremely popular *foie gras torchon*.

6 Pizzeria Delfina
MAP F5 ■ 2406 California St
■ (415) 440-1189 ■ $

Rustic, simple, and fresh, this
popular pizzeria serves incredible
Neapolitan thin-crust pizzas in
addition to delicious, traditional
antipasti and salami.

7 Spruce
MAP D3 ■ 3640 Sacramento St
■ (415) 931-5100 ■ $$$

One of the best restaurants in
the city, Spruce *(see p73)* offers
a seasonal meat-focused menu.

8 Udon Mugizo
MAP F3 ■ Japantown
Peace Plaza, 1581 Webster St
■ (415) 931-3118 ■ $

A cozy spot in Japantown serving a
variety of excellent noodles.

9 Blue Front Café
MAP E4 ■ 1430 Haight St
■ (415) 252-5917 ■ $

For cheap, tasty Mediterranean
wraps and sandwiches, this spot
is a local favorite.

10 Arizmendi
MAP F5 ■ 1272 Valencia St

This delightful cooperative *(see p74)*
serves delicious artisan breads and
a range of gourmet pizzas.

See map on p102

🔟 Southern Neighborhoods

The southern part of San Francisco comprises some of the liveliest parts of the city – the clubs of SoMa, the LGBTQ+ world of the Castro, and the Latin American Mission District. With high rents and real estate prices forcing lower-income residents out of the center and into the south, many of the neighborhoods on this side of the city have become popular with locals seeking more affordable housing. Noe Valley was the first such choice, but, gentrification there has pushed people further south to up-and-coming areas such as Bernal Heights and Glen Park.

Mission Dolores facade detail

SOUTHERN NEIGHBORHOODS

① Top 10 Sights
see pp109–11

① Places to Eat
see p115

① Shops
see p112

① Bars
see p114

① Nightclubs
see p113

① China Basin
MAP H4

This old shipping port area was revitalized with the addition of the Oracle Park, a venue for numerous concerts throughout the year, and home to the San Francisco Giants – the city's major league baseball team. Numerous restaurants and sports bars have

China Basin statue

opened up here. There are many entertainment options, including a bowling alley, which attract families and sports fans alike to this waterfront neighborhood.

② Mission Dolores
MAP F5 ■ 3321 16th St at Dolores St ■ (415) 621-8203 ■ Open 10am–4pm Tue–Sun ■ www. missiondolores.org

The Spanish Misión San Francisco de Asís, from which the city takes its name, is a marvel of preservation and atmospheric charm. It was founded in 1776, a few weeks before the Declaration of Independence.

③ South of Market
MAP R4

This former rough-and-tumble warehouse district *(see p35)* now houses high-tech offices. Some of the city's best eating joints, bars, and galleries are in SoMa.

④ Castro District
MAP E5

This neighborhood, with the historic Castro Theatre, is the center of the city's LGBTQ+ community. The intersection of Castro and 18th Streets is known as the "Gayest Four Corners of the World." This district emerged in the 1970s as a pilgrimage for gay travelers from all over the world. Every Halloween, Castro Street hosts a costume party and parade that is second to the San Francisco Pride parade *(see p81)*.

Castro Theatre

AN LGBTQ+-FRIENDLY CITY

After the free-love movement of the 1960s *(see p104)*, gay men were galvanized into organized political action. They started moving into the Castro in the 1970s. In no time, the neighborhood was a nonstop – and unstoppable – party of freewheeling sexual openness. Suddenly they were "out" in their relative legions, which brought with it political clout. San Francisco is still one of the easiest places in the world to live an openly LGBTQ+ lifestyle.

⑤ Yerba Buena Center

This is fast becoming one of San Francisco's leading centers *(see p34)* for the performing arts and has a growing number of museums representing the city's ethnic diversity. Every year sees some new addition to the complex.

⑥ San Francisco Museum of Modern Art

San Francisco's home for its extensive modern art collection *(see pp32–3)* is as impressive outside as it is awe-inspiring inside. Its expansive galleries enable a great amount of its stunning treasure of paintings, photography, media and digital installations, designs, and sculptures to be on show.

⑦ Noe Valley
MAP E6

Once a simple working-class neighborhood, until the 1970s brought hippies, LGBTQ+ community, and artists to its slopes and Noe Valley became an attractive alternative to more established quarters. In its hey-day it was known as both "Nowhere Valley" for its relative remoteness, and as "Granola Valley" for its nature-loving denizens. Lately, it has been taken over by middle-class professionals, who value it for its orderliness, but 24th Street still hums with activity and is lined with cafés and bookstores.

⑧ Moscone Center

Embellishing the SoMa cultural and business district, the Moscone Center *(see p34)* consists of an impressive central building, as well as a new, glass-enclosed expansion. The city's largest convention space also features an arrival plaza, enclosed bridges, and gardens, all connecting the massive three-block facility to surrounding hotels, theaters, restaurants, museums, and parks.

⑨ Mission District
MAP F5

The Mission *(see p80)* is home to much of the city's Latin American community.

San Francisco Museum of Modern Art

They have brought their culture and traditions with them – taquerías, salsa clubs, Santería shops, murals, and Spanish influences are found everywhere. Its festivals are not to be missed, especially Carnaval.

Carnaval parade, Mission District

🔟 Potrero Hill

MAP H5 ■ Anchor Brewing Co, 1705 Mariposa St ■ (415) 863-8350 ■ www.anchorbrewing.com

This SoMa hill was once set to become the next big thing, but its isolation kept that from happening, cut off from the rest of the city, as it is, by freeways on three sides and its own precipitous inclines. It has remained a quiet neighborhood with spectacular views. There are restaurants, bars, and many design stores here, but it is mostly residential. A noteworthy site is the Anchor Brewing Company. For $20 per person, you can participate in a tour and tasting session. There are only two or three tours a day, and it's best to book online in advance.

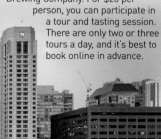

A WALK AROUND THE CASTRO DISTRICT

Begin at the LGBTQ+ hub of San Francisco, the Church Street Muni Station on Upper Market. Decades ago, this corner became the symbolic starting point of the Castro neighborhood, but it is on the next block, between Sanchez and Noe, that the LGBTQ+ shops and venues really begin to proliferate. Toward the corner of Castro is the popular nightclub The Café *(see p113)*, offering a range of strong drinks.

Continuing on to Castro Street, take in Harvey Milk Plaza *(see p45)*, with its huge rainbow flag; the plaza is named for the first openly gay politician elected to public office in California, who was assassinated in 1978. On the opposite corner, check out Twin Peaks *(see p71)*, the first gay bar in the country, notable for its street-facing windows, which allow passersby to see inside.

Pushing on to No. 429, allow the Castro Theatre to capture your attention. One of the city's most ornate cinema palaces, it hosts a number of premieres of films with LGBTQ+ themes. Farther along at No. 570, Brand X Antiques *(see p112)* is a great place to browse, with its eclectic collection of goods, ranging from furniture to homoerotica. On Hartford Street, Moby Dick *(see p70)* is a popular spot that attracts a steady crowd of regulars. Finish here to shoot some pool or pinball while enjoying 1980s tunes with a well-earned drink.

See map on pp108–9 ←

Shops

1 Needles & Pens
MAP F5 ▪ 1173 Valencia St
▪ (415) 872-9189
There's a little bit of everything at this funky, eclectic store. Don't miss the fantastic magazine selection, unique cards, stationery, and T-shirts, as well as the gallery.

2 WearSomethingRare
MAP R6 ▪ 440 Brannan St
▪ (415) 795-4105
Limited production clothing made on-site by local, talented designers. Watch your shirt being sewed in the factory at the back.

3 Borderlands Books
MAP E4 ▪ 1740 Haight St
▪ (415) 824-8203
A bookstore specializing in science fiction, horror, and fantasy. Whether these genres are your cup of tea or not, Borderlands is worth a visit for a dose of the unusual.

4 Brand X Antiques
MAP E5 ▪ 570 Castro St
▪ (415) 626-8908
The gay couple who own this shop share a discerning and humorous eye for antiques. In addition to baubles, rings, and furniture, the collection also features tongue-in-cheek vintage homoerotica.

5 Wink San Francisco
MAP E5 ▪ 4107 24th St
▪ (415) 401-8881
A large gift shop brimming with personality, thanks to a whimsical selection of eccentric books, toys, and home decor.

6 Wilkes Bashford
MAP P4 ▪ 375 Sutter St
Founded in 1966, Wilkes Bashford is a family-owned luxury clothing store *(see p76)* that styles San Francisco's elite. Wilkes Bashford stocks high-end designs, including fine footwear. The onsite tailor customizes any purchases as desired.

7 Creativity Explored
MAP F4 ▪ 3245 16th St
▪ (415) 863-2108 ▪ www.creativityexplored.org
Celebrating artists with developmental disabilities, this studio and gallery space has a shop selling the artists' works.

8 City Art Gallery
MAP F5 ▪ 828 Valencia St between 19th & 20th ▪ (415) 970-9900 ▪ Open noon–9pm Wed–Sun ▪ www.cityartgallery.org
This gallery *(see p52)* sells reasonably priced works of art, making it a great spot to find a unique gift.

9 Alexander Book Company
MAP P5 ▪ 50 Second St ▪ (415) 495-2992
Located near the Montgomery Street BART station, this bookstore *(see p76)* spans three floors and has all genres of literature, from children's books and classics, to coffee-table books and textbooks.

10 Paxton Gate
MAP F5 ▪ 824 Valencia St
▪ (415) 824-1872
This wonderland of unique items for gifts and home decor even includes strange pieces of taxidermy. Kids will love this place as much as adults do.

Glittering treasures at Paxton Gate

Nightclubs

1 Powerhouse
MAP G4 ▪ 1347 Folsom St
▪ (415) 552-8689 ▪ Closed Mon & Tue
One of the city's most popular, anything-goes gay leather bar, Powerhouse is a welcoming and safe space. The basic decor compliments the no-frills stiff drinks.

2 Make-Out Room
MAP F5 ▪ 3225 22nd St at
Mission ▪ (415) 647-2888
Live music and DJ nights make this a Mission favorite *(see p69)*. The decor is reasonably original and the drinks are reasonably priced.

3 The Café
MAP E5 ▪ 2369 Market St at
Castro ▪ (415) 523-0133
There is something (and somebody) for everybody at this camp, cruisy Castro old-timer that welcomes all. The outdoor balcony is great for people-watching.

4 AsiaSF
MAP G4 ▪ 201 9th St at
Howard ▪ (415) 255-2742
Brazen Asian drag queens are your waitresses, who also perform bartop and stage numbers. The tropical cocktails glow in the dark. There are DJs and dancing downstairs.

5 The EndUp
MAP R4 ▪ 401 6th St at
Harrison ▪ (415) 357-0827
Formerly exclusively gay, as famously featured in *Tales of the City* by Armistead Maupin *(see p55)*, this classic is now thoroughly mixed, featuring house music and an all-day Sunday "T" Dance.

6 500 Club
MAP F4 ▪ 500 Guerrero St
▪ (415) 861-2500
Cheap, stiff drinks, loud music, and plenty of seating space makes this place a trendy, local favorite. You cannot miss the neon sign that points to the entrance.

7 The Royale
MAP G2 ▪ 800 Post St
▪ (415) 441-4099 ▪ Closed Sun
This thriving club hosts everything from art exhibits to live jazz concerts. The bar offers a huge selection of wines and beers.

8 El Rio
MAP F5 ▪ 3158 Mission St
▪ (415) 282-3325
Different dance events organized every night of the week draw a diverse crowd ready to do their thing at this bar, which opened in 1978. Sunday Salsa Showcase is particularly popular.

Lively crowd at The Chapel

9 The Chapel
MAP F5 ▪ 777 Valencia St
▪ (415) 551-5157
Formerly a chapel, this place now showcases live music and comedy acts by local as well as national artists. Have dinner or drinks prior to the performance at the attached pub.

10 The Great Northern
MAP G4 ▪ 119 Utah St at 15th
▪ (415) 762-0151
Popular hip-hop and house DJs keep the crowds dancing at this large nightclub *(see p68)*, which also doubles as an art gallery.

See map on pp108–9

Bars

1 Café du Nord
MAP F4 ■ 2174 Market St
■ (415) 471-2969
Located in the landmark Swedish American building, this subterranean restaurant and cocktail bar is one of the smartest the city has to offer.

2 Bottom of the Hill
MAP G4 ■ 1233 17th St between Texas & Missouri ■ (415) 626-4455
This legendary live-music venue (see p68) features an assortment of punk, rock, and folk bands, plus a pleasant back patio for beer breaks.

3 Nihon Whisky Lounge
MAP F4 ■ 1779 Folsom at 14th St ■ (415) 552-4400
The white-pebbled floor and vast selection of hard-to-find whiskeys make this Japanese whiskey lounge a super-cool spot to grab a drink.

4 Rooftop 25
MAP H3 ■ 25 Lusk St ■ (415) 495-5875
Located in a renovated timber warehouse, this elegant bar-restaurant is sleek and modern with a hip, urban vibe. The cocktails are delicious and the stylish lounge below is great for people-watching.

5 Bourbon & Branch
MAP P3 ■ 501 Jones St ■ (415) 346-1735
This classy 1920s-style speakeasy (see p75) serves creative, cocktails using fresh ingredients. The secret rooms have a Prohibition-era atmosphere. Come here for hard-to-find liquors.

6 The Knockout
MAP F6 ■ 3223 Mission St ■ www.theknockoutsf.com
With DJs and live music all week, and bingo on Thursdays, The Knockout has remained one of the most popular dive bars in San Francisco for years.

The bright bar area at Trick Dog

7 Trick Dog
MAP F5 ■ 3010 20th St
■ (415) 471-2999
Well-crafted and imaginative cocktails win rave reviews at this beautiful, split-level bar in the Mission District. It has innovative decor and delicious bar snacks.

Rare whiskey, Nihon Whisky Lounge

8 DNA Lounge
MAP F4 ■ 375 11th St ■ (415) 626-1409
One of San Francisco's most popular party spots, this multi-level nightclub (see p68) and restaurant features an eclectic variety of live events such as electronic music, rock bands and DJ sets. It's the go-to place for local off-beat entertainment such as theater, burlesque, and spoken-word performances.

9 Hotel Utah Saloon
MAP R5 ■ 500 4th St ■ (415) 546-6300
This Gold-Rush-themed bar, with a honky-tonk atmosphere hosts live local music acts and has a long bar.

10 21st Amendment
MAP R6 ■ 563 2nd St ■ (415) 369-0900
A sports fan's dream, this brewpub near the ballpark serves up hand-crafted beers and standard American fare. It's a friendly place to catch a game on television.

Places to Eat

PRICE CATEGORIES

For a three-course meal for one with half a bottle of wine (or equivalent meal), taxes, and extra charges.

$ under $40 $$ $40–$80 $$$ over $80

1 Stable Café
MAP F5 ■ 2128 Folsom at 17th St ■ (415) 552-1199 ■ Closed D ■ $

Stable Café offers delicious homemade breakfast and lunch options that center on fresh-baked breads and healthy local ingredients.

2 Marlowe
MAP H3 ■ 500 Brannan St ■ (415) 777-1413 ■ $$

This cozy yet chic restaurant serves outstanding bistro dishes.

3 Prospect
MAP H2 ■ 300 Spear St ■ (415) 247-7770 ■ $$$

One of the city's most stand-out meals can be had at this SoMa mainstay. The decadent brunch is less pricey.

4 Tartine Bakery and Café
MAP F5 ■ 600 Guerrero St ■ (415) 487-2600 ■ $

The award-winning breads, cakes, and pastries here *(see p74)* draw a crowd. Get ready to wait in line.

5 Kitchen Story
MAP F4 ■ 3499 16th St ■ (415) 525-4905 ■ $$$

This restaurant offers excellent Asian-inspired Californian fare.

Arrive hungry to enjoy hearty portions of curries, seafood, and delicious veggie dishes.

6 Pancho Villa Taqueria
MAP F4 ■ 3071 16th St ■ (415) 864-8840 ■ $

This is one of the best Mexican restaurants in the city, serving authentic tacos and burritos for low prices.

7 Foreign Cinema
MAP F5 ■ 2534 Mission St ■ (415) 648-7600 ■ $$

Entertaining guests by screening old and new movies as they dine, Foreign Cinema *(see p72)* is a recurring name on the *San Francisco Chronicle*'s list of the city's top 100 restaurants.

8 Caffè Centro
MAP R6 ■ 102 South Park ■ (415) 882-1500 ■ Closed Sun ■ $

Drinks, pastries, soups, and salads are served at this bustling café.

9 El Farolito
MAP F5 ■ 2779 Mission St at 24th ■ www. elfarolitosf.com ■ $

Line up for superb tacos, generous Mission-style burritos, and other hot main dishes at this bright, buzzing place.

10 Delfina
MAP F5 ■ 3621 18th St ■ (415) 552-4055 ■ Closed L ■ $$

Delfina *(see p73)* serves perfect Italian fare. Its next-door pizzeria is ideal for a more casual dinner.

Sophisticated interior of Italian restaurant Delfina

See map on pp108–9

🔟 Oceanfront

As with every part of the city, this area is a study in contrasts. It contains terrains of natural, untamed beauty – particularly the windswept cliffs and hidden ravines of Land's End, the scene of innumerable shipwrecks. Yet, just a few blocks away is Sea Cliff, one of the most exclusive residential neighborhoods. Of all the city's areas, this is where you're almost certain to encounter the infamous fog, but if the weather is clear there are great views of the offshore Seal Rocks and even the Farallon Islands.

Statue at Legion of Honor

OCEANFRONT

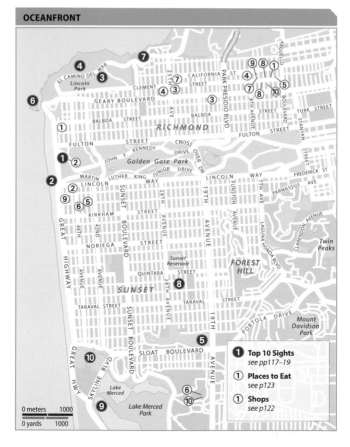

1 Top 10 Sights
see pp117–19

1 Places to Eat
see p123

1 Shops
see p122

0 meters 1000
0 yards 1000

1 Beach Chalet
MAP A4 ■ 1000 Great Highway ■ (415) 386-8439

This 1925 colonial-revival style building was originally the Golden Gate Park Chalet, before becoming an Army headquarters, and then a dive bar. It's now a spectacular place to eat. On the ground floor, the historic frescoes of life in San Francisco in the 1930s are a delight. Upstairs, the sweeping views of the beach and the crashing Pacific waves are enchanting, especially at sunset. The menu features an array of San Francisco staples like *cioppino* (fish stew) and ales and lagers crafted on site. There's also an excellent happy hour menu.

2 Ocean Beach
MAP A4 ■ The Great Hwy

Most of the western boundary of San Francisco is defined by this broad sweep of sand. Although it is a sublime sight when viewed from Cliff House or Sutro Heights Park, do note that the beach is dangerous to swim from due to its icy waters, rough shore breakers, and, most of all, rip currents that are powerful enough to drag even strong swimmers out to sea. Nevertheless, hardy Californian surfers in thick wetsuits are a common sight here, and in fine weather sunbathers and picnickers materialize to loll on the sand and enjoy the sunshine.

3 Legion of Honor
MAP B3 ■ 100 34th Avenue, Lincoln Park ■ (415) 750-3600 ■ Open 9:30am–5:15pm Tue–Sun ■ Adm ■ www.famsf.org

The creation of Alma de Bretteville Spreckels, heiress to the Spreckels sugar fortune, this museum is a replica of the Palais de la Légion d'Honneur in Paris. The original structure was built for the 1915 Panama-Pacific Exposition, but Mrs. Spreckels wanted to build a permanent version and employed the same architect she commissioned for her mansion in Pacific Heights *(see p103)*. It opened in 1924 and features medieval to 20th-century European art, with paintings by Monet and Rembrandt. The museum also hosts excellent traveling exhibitions.

4 Oceanfront Parks
MAP A3

Lincoln Park, Lands End, and Sutro Heights Park are large green areas overlooking the coast along this northwestern corner of the peninsula. Lincoln Park is the work of John McClaren *(see p25)*, and has trails with some of the best views of the Golden Gate Bridge. Lands End is a rugged stretch along the cliffs that features a picturesque cove and spectacular hiking. Statuary of the old Sutro estate still decorates Sutro Heights Park, which dominates the coastal scene from its vantage point.

Rock labyrinth by Eduardo Aguilera at Lands End

5 Sigmund Stern Recreation Grove

Sloat Blvd at 19th Ave, Sunset ▪ (415) 252-6252 ▪ www.sterngrove.org

This 33-acre (13-ha) ravine *(see p57)* in the southern Sunset District was donated to the city of San Francisco by Rosalie M. Stern in 1931, in memory of her husband Sigmund, a civic leader. It is the site of the nation's original free summer arts festival, Stern Grove Festival, which was endowed in 1938 and is still in operation today. Running on Sunday afternoons, the program may include classical music performed by the San Francisco Symphony Orchestra, opera, jazz, popular music, or productions by the San Francisco Ballet. The natural amphitheater, in a eucalyptus, fir, and redwood grove, has great acoustics.

6 Seal Rocks

MAP A3

The westernmost promontory on this tip of the peninsula is Point Lobos, the projection that forms the rocky cove of Land's End. Along to the south from here down to Cliff House is a scattering of small, rocky islands that are frequented by seals – hence the name. Bring binoculars with you to spy on the seals and birds in their natural habitat. At night, from the beach or Cliff House promenade, the barking of the sea lions – like the keening of the foghorns – is both reassuring and eerie, and so very "San Francisco." On a clear day, 32 miles (50 km) off the coast, you can see the Farallon Islands, which are also inhabited by sea lions and have a state-protected rookery.

Seals basking on the Seal Rocks

CLIFF HOUSE AND THE SUTRO BATHS

Adolph Sutro came to San Francisco from Prussia in 1851, aged 21 and looking for gold. He became "King of the Comstock Lode" in Nevada, and brought his riches back to the city to invest them in land. His projects included building the first Cliff House, the popular Sutro Baths, and his own lavish estate. In the process, he made the Ocean Beach area into a recreational gem. The legacy lives on, despite the disappearance of all three of the famous buildings he constructed.

7 Sea Cliff

MAP C2

Many famous residents, such as Twitter founder Jack Dorsey and actress Sharon Stone, have had homes in this elite residential enclave, which stands in stark contrast to the natural coastal area all around it. Most of the luxurious homes are Mediterranean in style and date from the 1920s. Just below the neighborhood, China Beach *(see p58)*, which was named after poor Chinese fishers who used to camp here, is one of the safest beaches in the city for swimming and is equipped with showers and other facilities. Baker Beach *(see p59)*, just to the north, is another popular beach.

8 Sunset District

MAP C5 ▪ West-central San Francisco, between Sloat Blvd & Golden Gate Park

Like its counterpart, the Richmond District *(see p104)*, this neighborhood was part of the Outer Lands and is

purely residential, consisting of row upon row of neat, lookalike houses. Yet, like the entire area along the ocean, this district is subject to a great deal of gray weather. Its one claim to fame is Sutro Tower, the pronged red-and-white television antenna that resembles something out of a science fiction movie.

9 Lake Merced
Hwy 35

Located at the beginning of scenic Skyline Boulevard (Hwy 35), this lake, set amid verdant hills, extends across the southern end of the Sunset District. Relatively undeveloped and underused, it nevertheless gets its share of recreation enthusiasts. They come for the municipal 18-hole TPC Harding Park golf course, as well as the biking and running trails that circle the lake's green shoreline.

Fishing boats on Lake Merced

10 San Francisco Zoo
Sloat Blvd at Pacific Ocean
■ Buses 18 & 23 ■ (415) 753-7080
■ Open 10am–5pm (last entry 4pm)
daily ■ Adm ■ www.sfzoo.org

San Francisco Zoo is at the far southwest corner of the city, between the Pacific Ocean and Lake Merced. The complex is home to more than 1,000 species. Gorilla Preserve, Grizzly Gulch, Koala Crossing, and Children's Zoo are particular hits, as are the feeding times for the grizzly bears and the penguins. Summer brings a busy program of extra activities in the Children's Zoo.

A TWO-HOUR HIKE AROUND LAND'S END

This section of the coast is amazingly wild, especially considering that it is actually within the city limits. Note that portions of the hike are very rugged, so dress accordingly, with sturdy footwear.

Begin at the far end of the Merrie Way parking lot and take the steps down. Follow the trail that passes by the Sutro Baths ruins, to your left as you descend. Continue on along to the Overlook, from which you can take in **Seal Rocks** and much of the Pacific panorama.

Now double back a bit to pick up the trail that continues along the coast. You will see the remains of concrete military bunkers, which have been broken and tilted by the unstable land, and are now decorated with graffiti. Soon you will come to a beach below rocky cliffs; note that the surging water is very unpredictable here, so be very careful. Continue walking and you will arrive at Land's End Cove, where a makeshift beach, using rock walls as windbreakers, is popular with nudists.

Next, climb up one of the sets of wooden steps to join the path up above and continue on around the bend, where a stunning view of the **Golden Gate Bridge** *(see pp12–13)* will greet you. Continue walking all the way to Eagle's Point and then return by way of the higher trail that winds through **Lincoln Park** *(see p117)*.

If you have worked up an appetite from your hike, enjoy a meal and the wonderful views at **Louis'** *(902 Point Lobos Ave; www.louissf.com)*, located nearby.

See map on p116

Shops

(1) Park Life
MAP D3 ▪ 220 Clement St
▪ (415) 386-7275
Part retail store, part art gallery,
this sleek space features limited-
edition books, prints, homeware,
jewelry, T-shirts, and art. The
gallery exhibits contemporary art.

(2) The Last Straw
MAP A5 ▪ 4540 Irving St
▪ (415) 566-4692
This tiny store near the beach
has been run by the same friendly
owner for more than 30 years. Great,
interesting pieces of jewelry and
unique finds are on sale here.

**(3) Gaslight & Shadows
Antiques**
MAP C3 ▪ 2335 Clement St
▪ (415) 387-0633
The specialty here is porcelain,
specifically the delicate master-
pieces turned out by the various
makers in the town of Limoges,
France. It's like visiting a museum
dedicated to this fine art form. There
are dolls and costume jewelry, too.

(4) Paul's Hat Works
MAP B3 ▪ 6128 Geary Blvd
▪ (415) 221-5332
This one-of-a-kind store is devoted
to old-fashioned hat making. Each
hat is custom-made.

Custom-made hats at Paul's Hat Works

(5) Aqua Surf Shop
MAP A5 ▪ 3847 Judah St
▪ (415) 242-9283
Every sort of surf gear, including
the extra-thick wetsuits needed
to survive these northern waters.

(6) Stonestown Galleria
3251 20th Ave at Winston
Drive ▪ (415) 564-8848
Upmarket Nordstrom and
all-purpose Macy's are the
anchor stores in this traditional
indoor-outdoor shopping center
with the usual array of mall stores,
from Gap to Sunglass Hut, as
well as plenty of food outlets.

(7) Green Apple Books
MAP D3 ▪ 506 Clement St
▪ (415) 387-2272
It's easy to lose a few hours
browsing through the selection
of used books and DVDs at this
store. Part of the fun is taking the
time to read the well-written and
helpful staff recommendations.

(8) Foggy Notion
MAP D3 ▪ 124 Clement St
▪ (415) 683-5654
A eco-conscious boutique store
that specializes in handmade
home and health products,
ranging from body oils to scented
candles inspired by the coast
of California.

(9) Kamei Housewares
MAP D3 ▪ 547 Clement St
▪ (415) 666-3688
This large store has essential
equipment for cooking Asian
cuisines, and a wonderful selection
of tableware and tea sets.

(10) See's Candies
3251 20th Ave, Stonestown
Galleria ▪ (415) 731-1784
Founded in 1921 by Charles See,
this traditional shop offers high-
quality chocolates, truffles,
brittles, toffees, and lollipops.

Previous pages Golden Gate Bridge and Fort Point

Places to Eat

PRICE CATEGORIES
For a three-course meal for one with half a bottle of wine (or equivalent meal), taxes, and extra charges.

$ under $40 $$ $40–$80 $$$ over $80

1 TJ Café
MAP A4 ▪ **724 La Playa St**
▪ **(415) 702-6286** ▪ **$**

This café serves simple and delicious American bites, as well as fish and chips, which you can easily take with you to enjoy at the nearby Ocean Beach.

2 Beach Chalet Brewery
MAP A4 ▪ **1000 Great Hwy**
▪ **(415) 386-8439** ▪ **$$**

People come to this charming venue for the views – both of the ocean and the murals – as well as for the food.

3 Kabuto Sushi
MAP C3 ▪ **5121 Geary Blvd at 15th Ave** ▪ **(415) 752-5652** ▪ **Closed Mon** ▪ **$$**

A great Japanese restaurant – the sashimi melts in the mouth.

4 Good Luck Dim Sum
MAP D3 ▪ **736 Clement St**
▪ **(415) 386-3388** ▪ **$**

This tiny place has a wide selection of inexpensive dim sum. The chive and shrimp dumplings are especially good. Perfect for take out.

5 Chapeau!
MAP C3 ▪ **126 Clement St at 2nd Ave** ▪ **(415) 750-9787**
▪ **Closed L** ▪ **$$**

A memorably quaint French bistro. The sommelier can direct you to fine wines that pair well with the classic fare, which includes *filet mignon*.

6 Outerlands
MAP A3 ▪ **4001 Judah St**
▪ **(415) 661-6140** ▪ **$**

Grab a table outside, or enjoy the rustic interior, here. Feast on the creative,

Brunch dishes at Outerlands

organic-based menus, offering fresh seafood, veggie soups and sandwiches, along with salads. They serve great cocktails, too. Come early for the popular Sunday brunch.

7 Pizzetta 211
MAP C3 ▪ **211 23rd Ave**
▪ **(415) 379-9880** ▪ **$**

Thin and crisp pizza topped with organic ingredients from fragrant aioli to homemade sausage.

8 Café Bunn Mi
MAP D3 ▪ **417 Clement St**
▪ **(415) 668-8908** ▪ **$**

Vietnamese sandwiches at their best, and for a bargain, too.

9 Java Beach Café
MAP A5 ▪ **1396 La Playa St**
▪ **(415) 665-5282** ▪ **$**

This cozy café serves sandwiches, soup, and pastries in a nautical-themed interior.

10 Burma Superstar
MAP D3 ▪ **309 Clement St**
▪ **(415) 387-2147** ▪ **$**

This Burmese restaurant features an extensive menu of flavorsome noodles, curries, and salads.

See map on p116

TOP10 The Bay Area

In local parlance, the Bay Area includes the City, the East Bay, Marin, the Peninsula, and the South Bay. Although Santa Clara, San Jose, Santa Cruz, and Capitola do not touch the waters of the Bay, they embody the same open-minded ethos that defines it. This is largely due to Northern California's well-known liberal population and diverse community. In towns such as Berkeley the emphasis is on progressive thinking, while smaller enclaves such as Bolinas live life in harmony with the breathtaking nature all around them.

Oakland's Paramount Theatre

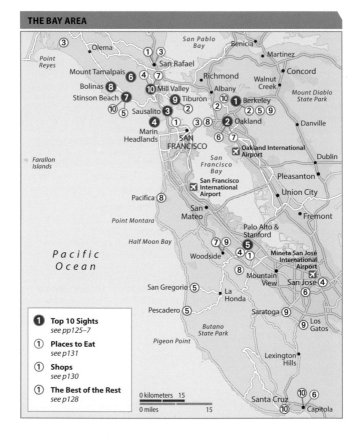

THE BAY AREA

- **1** Top 10 Sights
  see pp125–7
- ① Places to Eat
  see p131
- ① Shops
  see p130
- ① The Best of the Rest
  see p128

0 kilometers   15

0 miles   15

Houseboats in the former fishing community of Sausalito

1 Berkeley
BART Downtown Berkeley

Known as "Berzerkeley," for the student dissent of the 1960s, today the tree-shaded UC Berkeley campus is still the center of TV-worthy protests. As one of the world's greatest universities, "Cal's" faculty features many Nobel laureates. This diversity-proud East Bay city is full of gourmet cafés and a variety of restaurants. Fourth street is sprinkled with shops, while the parks, as well as the biking and hiking trails appeal to those wishing to escape the bustle of city life.

2 Oakland
BART 12th St

Notorious for civic unrest and crime in the past, Oakland is now a multicultural haven for artists, musicians, and those fleeing the high rents of San Francisco. The city's attractions include the huge Lake Merritt, which offers a range of recreational possibilities, the Oakland Museum of California (see p129), the Oakland Zoo, two glorious Art Deco-era theaters (Paramount and Fox), the Jack London Square waterfront complex of restaurants and shops, the USS Potomac (FDR's Floating White House), and a ferry landing. In the hills, you will find a beautiful Mormon Temple, with dazzling Bay views, the Redwood Regional Park, and the Chabot Space and Science Center.

3 Sausalito
US 101

A former fishing community and now an upscale commuter area and tourist haven, this small town offers spectacular views of San Francisco from its Bridgeway Avenue promenade. Historically, it has been an artists' town, home to an eccentric mix of residents. Bungalows cling to the hillsides and boats fill the picturesque marinas, many of them are houseboats that locals live in year-round. There are excellent restaurants, places to stay, and some unique shopping possibilities, too.

4 Marin Headlands
Muni Bus 76

To visit these raw, wild hills with astonishingly beautiful views is to enter another world; yet it's only half an hour's drive from the city, via the Golden Gate Bridge. The scale of the rolling terrain is immense, and the precipitous drops into the ocean are dramatic. This is an unspoiled area of wildlife (Point Reyes to the north is home to tule elk herds), windswept ridges, sheltered valleys, and deserted beaches (see p58).

Tule elk, Point Reyes

The beautiful campus of Stanford University, Palo Alto

5 Palo Alto and Stanford
Hwys 101 & 82

An erstwhile sleepy university town, Palo Alto has experienced a boom as the focal point of Silicon Valley, and driving force of the "New Economy." Although the area has seen a rise in homelessness due to the increased cost of living, this town has been left with a considerably dressed-up appearance, as well as many fancy restaurants, hotels, and shops. The town is home to the prestigious private Stanford University *(see p83)*, with its beautiful, well-tended campus.

GREAT BAY AREA UNIVERSITIES

Palo Alto's Stanford University is the Bay Area's most famous private institution of higher learning, inaugurated in 1891. However, in terms of intellectual clout, the University of California at Berkeley, the oldest campus in the California system, stands shoulder to shoulder, considering the number of Nobel laureates on the faculty and its international importance. Stanford is known for business, law, and medicine, while Berkeley is famed for law, engineering, and nuclear physics. Both universities are among the most selective in the entire country.

---

6 Mount Tamalpais
Hwy 1

From the summit of 2,570-ft (785-m) "Mount Tam," sacred to the Native Americans who once lived here, practically the entire Bay Area can be seen. The area is a state park, with more than 200 miles (320 km) of trails through redwood groves and alongside creeks. There are picnic areas, campsites, an open-air theater, and meadows for kite flying.

Mountain Theatre, Mount Tamalpais

7 Stinson Beach
Hwy 1

Since the early 20th century, this *(see p58)* has been a popular vacation spot and remains the preferred swimming beach for the whole area. The soft sand and the spectacular sunsets set off the quaint village, with its good restaurants and interesting shops. You can reach it via the coast route, but the drive up Highway 1 gives the most dramatic arrival, with inspiring views as you exit the forest onto the headlands.

8 Bolinas
Hwy 1

Bolinas is a hippie village that time forgot. The citizens regularly take down road signs showing the way to downtown, to keep away visitors. Potters and other craftspeople sell their wares in the funky gallery, organic produce and vegetarianism are the rule, and 1960s idealism still predominates.

"Ark Row" shops, Tiburon

9 Tiburon
Hwy 131

Marin County's less hectic alternative to Sausalito – here, 100-year-old houseboats ("arks") have been pulled ashore and refurbished, forming "Ark Row." It houses shops, restaurants, and cafés that enhance the charm of this waterfront village. There are also opportunities to see wildlife in the parks along the shore, facing Angel Island and the city.

10 Mill Valley
Off Hwy 101

Home to a well-known film festival, this is the quintessential Marin town; wealthy, relaxed, beautiful, and with a well-educated populace given to opinions on just about every topic. The old part of town is flanked by redwoods, lined with old buildings housing restaurants and unusual shops, and the whole centers around an eternally pleasant public square.

A MORNING WALK AROUND BERKELEY

Begin at UC Berkeley's **Koret Visitor Center** on Piedmont Avenue at Bancroft Way, where you can pick up information and maps. Continue on Piedmont Ave to the **Hearst Greek Theater**, an excellent concert venue. Then go left on University Drive; on your left, you'll shortly come across the Campanile Esplanade, which leads to the main campus landmark, the 307-ft (94-m) **Sather Tower**, also known simply as the Campanile, based on the famous bell tower in Venice's Piazza San Marco.

From the tower, Campanile Way leads to Harmon Way, bringing you to the neo-Romanesque **Wellman Hall**. From here, University Drive and then Crescent Lawn follow along the Eucalyptus Grove or Grinnel Natural area. Cross Oxford to find the **Berkeley Art Museum and Pacific Film Archive**. Head back through the Eucalyptus Grove to Fran Schelssinger Way. A roundabout will take you to Grade Street and then Sather's Cross Path, leading to Sather Gate and then into **Sproul Plaza**, epicenter of the student Free Speech Movement of the 1960s. Exit the campus onto Telegraph Avenue, a kind of East Bay Haight-Ashbury. One block over is **People's Park**.

After your walk, head over to **The Cheese Board Collective** *(1512 Shattuck Ave at Vine St; (510) 549-3183)*. The restaurant serves one type of vegetarian pizza a day, and it is known for its wide selection of rare cheeses.

See map on p124 ←

The Best of the Rest

1 San Rafael
Hwy 101

This town has a charming historic center with good restaurants and shops. A street market transforms the main drag into a bustling hub every Thursday evening.

2 Belvedere Island
This garden island, attached by a causeway to Tiburon, is one of the Bay's most exclusive residential areas. Worth a visit to see the palatial homes and their sumptuous setting.

3 Point Reyes
Hwy 1 to Olema, then signposted to Point Reyes

This windswept peninsula is a haven for wildlife, including a herd of tule elk; it is also home to cattle ranches. You can watch migrating whales offshore from December to March.

4 San Jose
Hwy 101

This sprawling town is an integral part of Silicon Valley enterprises and has popular attractions.

5 San Gregorio and Pescadero
Hwy 1

Sheltered by cliffs, San Gregorio Private Beach is the Bay Area's oldest nude beach. It is adjacent to the Pescadero State Beach, which has lots of tide pools. The fishing village evokes the Old West, complete with a white-washed wooden church. Duarte's Tavern has been serving artichoke soup and olallieberry pie since 1894.

Lighthouse, Pescadero

The bizzare Winchester Mystery House

6 Winchester Mystery House
525 S Winchester Blvd, San Jose
■ (408) 247-2000 ■ Open daily
(call for tour times) ■ Adm

The eccentric 19th-century home of the rifle heiress, Sarah Winchester, took 38 years to build and includes stairways leading to nowhere and windows set into floors.

7 Woodside
Hwy 280

This bucolic residential area is where many of the first families to have lived in the Bay Area built fabulous mansions in the late 19th century.

8 Pacifica
Hwy 1 off Hwy 280

A popular weekend destination, this oceanfront city is great for surfing, fishing, cycling, golf, and hiking. Lodgings and seafood restaurants face the ocean and the quaint little downtown is lined with shops.

9 Los Gatos and Saratoga
Hwy 85

These tree-lined small towns, full of restaurants and shops, have become upscale communities for the movers and shakers of Silicon Valley.

10 Santa Cruz and Capitola
Hwy 1

Some of the Central Coast's best swimming, plus the Boardwalk, a famous vintage amusement park.

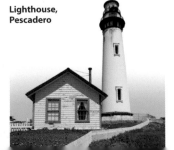

Oakland Museum of California

1 Earthquake Artifacts
A collection of objects that pertain to the terrible earthquake of 1906 are on display here, including porcelain cups and saucers fused together by the heat of the fire that destroyed so much of the city.

2 Natural Sciences
In the brilliant Gallery of California Natural Sciences, the state is presented as one of the world's top ten biological "hot spots." There are thousands of artifacts on display, including bird and mammal study skins and mounts, as well as an enormous collection of reptiles, amphibians, and fungi.

3 Mission-era Artifacts
A 19th-century icon of St. Peter is just one remnant of the Spanish Mission years you'll find here, where there are also colonial tools, and part of a Spanish ship.

4 The Earliest Californians
Fascinating galleries explore early human history in the state of California, documented by materials such as basketry, stone tools, clothing, and objects used in rituals.

5 Gold Rush Artifacts
The lives of those who came to California from all over the world in the 19th century, hoping to strike it rich, are chronicled here. You'll see gold nuggets, prospecting tools and rare mining equipment.

6 Californian History
This section of the museum has exhibits associated with technology, agriculture, business, and domestic life from the early Native Americans up to the 21st century. Subjects such as World War II, baby boomers, Hollywood, and Silicon Valley are also covered.

7 The Building
The museum building is an outstanding example of modern design. Opened in 1969, it is composed of reinforced concrete and consists of three levels of tiered terraces. To soften the angularity, roof gardens have been planted, accented with sculpture.

Oakland Museum of California

8 Art Gallery
The third level of the museum is devoted to the Gallery of California Art, featuring works by artists who have studied, lived, and worked here. Included are works by California Impressionists and members of the Bay Area Figurative Movement. Check the website (www.museumca.org) for the opening times of the California Art and History Galleries.

9 Photography
The Gallery of California Art also has an impressive collection of the work of California photographers, including Ansel Adams, Edward Weston, and Dorothea Lange.

Gold nugget

10 Californian Crafts
This is the largest collection in the world of work by California Arts and Crafts practitioners Arthur and Lucia Kleinhans Mathews, including paintings, drawings, furniture, and other decorative art.

See map on p124

Shops

1 Stanford Shopping Center

660 Stanford Shopping Center, Palo Alto ■ Hwy 101 ■ (650) 617-8200
One of the first shopping centers in the Bay Area, this outdoor mall is dog-friendly and features shops that you don't tend to find everywhere, such as Kate Spade, Free People, and Bloomingdales.

2 Favor

1649 San Pablo Avenue, Berkeley ■ www.shopatfavor.com
Beautifully carved resin jewelry and exclusive hotcake designs by designer Caramia are stocked at Favor along with works from designers across the globe.

3 Gene Hiller

729 Bridgeway Ave, Sausalito ■ Hwy 101 ■ (415) 332-3636
Since 1953, this menswear store has been offering the finest imported designer clothing – from classic formal to casual – including Ermenegildo Zegna and Canali.

4 Shady Lane

325 Sharon Park Drive, Menlo Park ■ Off Hwy 280 ■ (650) 321-1099
This boutique was founded by a collective of artists who wanted to create a showcase for their designs in areas like jewelry and ceramics.

Shady Lane at Sharon Park Drive

5 Moe's Books

2476 Telegraph Ave, Berkeley ■ (510) 849-2087
Opened by Moe Moskowitz in 1959, Moe's Books offers an excellent selection of new, used, and rare books.

6 Oaklandish

1444 Broadway, Oakland ■ (510) 251-9500
Established as a public art project in 2000, Oaklandish creates unqiue clothing while supporting the local community.

7 Margaret O'Leary

14 Miller Ave, Mill Valley ■ Off Hwy 101 ■ (415) 388-2390
Mill Valley is home to the flagship store of this women's knitwear label, known for its classic, upscale takes on California comfort.

8 Heath Ceramics

500 Gate 5 Rd, Sausalito ■ Off Hwy 101 ■ (415) 332-3732
An iconic Bay Area ceramics studio and store, Heath Ceramics features mid-century modern dinnerware, home accents, and imperfect factory pieces sold at reduced rates.

9 Fourth Street

Berkeley ■ (510) 644-3002
A tree-shaded warren of boutiques and galleries, this popular street is lined by the likes of The Gardener, Sur La Table, Stained Glass Garden, Builders Booksource, and Jeffrey's Toys.

10 Claudia Chapline Gallery and Sculpture Garden

3445 Shoreline Hwy, Stinson Beach ■ Hwy 1 ■ (415) 868-2308
The Chapline sculpture garden is impressive, especially Lyman Whitaker's brilliant kinetic pieces, which are driven by the wind. Inside, the variety and quality of painted and mixed-media work is very compelling.

Places to Eat

PRICE CATEGORIES
For a three-course meal for one with half a bottle of wine (or equivalent meal), taxes, and extra charges.

$ under $40 $$ $40–$80 $$$ over $80

1 Poggio Trattoria
777 Bridgeway, Sausalito
■ (415) 332-7771 ■ $$

Overlooking the waterfront, this *trattoria* serves award-winning Northern Italian food. There is also a list of fabulous cocktails on offer. Grab a booth or a sidewalk table.

2 Viks Chaat
2390 Fourth Street, Berkeley
■ (510) 644-4432 ■ $

This big, lively restaurant attached to a South Asian grocery store serves excellent Indian street food.

3 Sol Food
901 Lincoln Ave, San Rafael
■ Hwy 101 ■ (415) 451-4765 ■ $

Line up for a taste of the flavorful, festive Puerto Rican food at this restaurant. There is a special dish on the menu, which changes every day.

4 The Depot Café and Bookstore
87 Throckmorton Ave, Mill Valley
■ (415) 888-3648 ■ $

This bookstore, with its renowned café, offers regular author events as well as phenomenal paninis.

5 Parkside Snack Bar
43 Arenal Ave, Stinson Beach
■ Hwy 1 ■ (415) 868-1272 ■ $

Creative brunch at picnic tables on the patio, or in the dining room. Try the Tomales Bay mussels.

6 Gayle's Bakery & Rosticceria
504 Bay Ave, Capitola ■ Hwy 1
■ (831) 462-1200 ■ $

This bakery and *rosticceria* (or deli) features an extraordinary selection

A selection of cakes at Gayle's

of gourmet treats, both sweet and savory. Try the Opera Cake and the to-die-for cupcakes.

7 Café Eritrea d'Afrique
4069 Telegraph Ave, Oakland
■ Hwy 880 ■ (510) 547-4520 ■ $

An acclaimed restaurant serving Eritrean and Ethiopian cuisine in a relaxing and friendly atmosphere. They offer an all-you-can-eat veggie buffet on Wednesdays and Fridays.

8 Alpine Inn
3915 Alpine Rd, Portola Valley
■ Hwy 280 ■ (650) 854-4004 ■ $

In a building that dates back to 1850, this greasy beer bar with a garden is popular with locals and Silicon Valley workers alike for its substantial burgers and fries.

9 Buck's
3062 Woodside Drive, Woodside ■ Hwy 280 ■ (650) 851-8010 ■ $

After a long hike on one of the many trails in Woodside, enjoy a hearty Woodsider omelet and coffee at this kitsch restaurant.

10 Chez Panisse
1517 Shattuck Ave, Berkeley
■ Hwy 80 ■ (510) 548-5525
■ Closed Sun ■ $$$

A popular Berkeley spot *(see p73)* has been serving up excellent California cuisine, using organic seasonal ingredients, since 1971. The upstairs café offers a cheaper alternative.

See map on p124 ←

Streetsmart

**The crooked turns of
Lombard Street**

Getting Around

Arriving by Air

Three international airports serve the San Francisco Bay Area, all linked by public transportation to one another.
San Francisco International Airport (SFO) is 14 miles (23 km) south of the city. It is one of the world's busiest airports, with over 40 international airlines operating here. However, it is also one of the most user-friendly.

The airport's Bay Area Rapid Transit (BART) station is connected to the terminals by a light-rail shuttle (although it stops frequently, so allow time for the journey). BART connects to four Downtown stations, and to **Caltrain**, which connects to San Jose.

Rental cars, taxis, limousines, and shuttles to surrounding cities and Downtown hotels are available at the airport. There are some minibus companies, such as **SuperShuttle**, that offer a door-to-door shuttle service, taking passengers to a specific address. The cost of the trip is shared with the other passengers. A taxi ride from SFO into the city averages at about $56 plus tip.
Oakland International Airport (OAK) is about an hour's bus ride across the bay across the Bay from San Francisco. There is good transportation into San Francisco by door-to-door bus, car, and limousine shuttle services. The airport

is served by BART and connects to four San Francisco stations.
Mineta San Jose International Airport (SJC), in the heart of Silicon Valley, is 45 miles (72 km) south of San Francisco. **SamTrans** provides a 24-hour bus service to the city and San Mateo County. BART and Caltrain also provide transport from SJC into San Francisco.

Train Travel

Amtrak trains link most major US cities. Advance booking is recommended for travel during peak periods.Those visiting San Francisco by train will arrive at the Amtrak station in Emeryville, to the north of Oakland. From here, a shuttle takes you to Mission Street in downtown San Francisco.

Alternatively, you can travel by Amtrak to San Jose, then transfer via the **CalTrain** commuter rail system to San Francisco. A separate ticket is required for this journey. The CalTrain stops near several Muni bus and Metro stops.

Long-Distance Bus Travel

For travelers on a budget and with more time, buses are a great way to travel. The **Greyhound** bus line takes passengers from Los Angeles to San Francisco in around 9 hours from $38. Discounts are offered for online purchases, 14-day

advance purchases, students, seniors, children, and large groups. The **Green Tortoise** bus company offers a friendly and adventurous way to see California, often stopping at tourist sights.

Public Transportation

San Francisco has a reliable and easy-to-use public transportation system run by the San Francisco Municipal Transportation Agency (**SFMTA**). The city's bus and Metro network is known as the Muni and covers buses, light rail Metro trains, streetcars (electric trams), and cable cars. The San Francisco Peninsula and the East Bay are linked by the Bay Area Rapid Transit (**BART**). This is an efficient way to get to both SFO and Oakland International Airport. Safety and hygiene measures, timetables, ticket information, transport maps, and more can be obtained from the SFMTA website. A **Clipper Card** gives you access to all information and digital tickets, and the app can be downloaded and used on a smart phone.

Planning Your Journey

Public transportation is busiest at 7am–9am and 4pm–7pm from Monday through Friday. The cable cars are a popular tourist activity, so are busy during the summer months.

The Muni Metro runs from around 5am to 1am on weekdays, from 7am on Saturdays and 8am on Sundays. There are ten Muni Owl services that run 24 hours a day, 7 days a week. Schedules are modified for public holidays, so check the SFMTA website before travelling.

Tickets

You can purchase a reusable Clipper card from Muni Metro stations, online, or from Walgreens stores for just $3. Top up the card with money and hold it against the reader when boarding a vehicle. You can use it to travel on the Muni, BART, and the cable cars.

Buses and streetcars are $2.50 ($3 by cash, exact change only) for two hours of travel. You can save up to $0.50 per trip by paying with a Clipper card (under-18s free).

Muni passports are available for 1, 3, or 7 days, allowing unlimited travel on buses, the Metro, streetcars, and cable cars. These can be purchased from the Visitor Information Center, the kiosk at San Francisco airport, and at other stores throughout the city.

Buses

There are bus stops every two or three blocks. Bus shelters list the route number of the buses that stop there, as well as maps and service frequency information. Most have digital signs showing when the next bus will arrive. Route numbers followed by a letter are either express services or make limited stops. You can pay with exact change, or show your Muni Passport or Clipper Card.

Metro

The Metro light rail system operates both above and below ground, and is another great way to see the city. Lines J (Church), K (Ingleside), L (Taraval), M (Ocean View), N (Judah), and T (Third) share the same tracks, so check the letter and name of the vehicle when boarding from Market Street. To go west, follow signs indicating "Outbound"; to go east, chooose "Downtown."

Streetcars

The F line streetcar runs along Market Street only, and features vintage streetcars from all over the world.

Cable Cars

San Francisco's cable cars are world-famous, and even classed as a "moving national monument". Service runs every ten minutes from 6am to midnight daily; the fare is $5 (over 5s) per journey, with a discount for seniors and those with disabilities after 9pm and before 7am. There are three routes: the Powell-Hyde line, which passes Union Square and climbs Nob Hill, providing good views of Chinatown. The Powell-Mason line begins in the same place and branches off to pass North Beach, ending at Bay Street. (Sit facing east for the best views)

The California line runs from the base of Market Street at the Embarcadero, through the Financial District and Chinatown, over Nob Hill, ending at Van Ness Avenue. You are more likely to get a seat if you board the cable car at the end of the line, but you may find it more fun to hang onto a pole while standing on a side running board.

BART

BART trains run from 5am on weekdays, from 6am on Saturdays, and from 8am on Sundays, until around midnight. Tickets are issued by machines in BART stations, which take cards or cash. You must present your ticket at the turnstile both when you board and leave the train. You can also use a Clipper card. The final destination of the train will be displayed on the front of the train itself, and the direction of travel will be marked on the platform.

Taxis

Taxis in San Francisco operate 24 hours a day. They are licensed and regulated, so expect efficient service, expert local knowledge, and a set price. A taxi will have its rooftop sign illuminated if vacant. It will also display the company name and telephone number, plus the cab number. Make a note of this, and if you leave anything in the cab, call the company and quote the cab number.

To catch a cab, wait at a taxi stand, call and request a pick-up, or hail a vacant cab. Tell your driver your exact destination. The meter will be on the dashboard; expect to add a 15 to 20 per cent tip to the final amount. Fares are often posted inside the cab. There is usually a flat fee of around $4.15 for the first mile (1.6 km). This increases by about $3.25 for each additional mile, or 65 cents per minute while waiting. Fares from the Ferry Building to the west coast

beaches are about $45. The driver will write you a receipt on request. If you travel 15 miles (24 km) or more beyond the city limits, the fare will be 150 per cent of the metered rate.

The taxi companies **Uber** and **Lyft** are very cost-effective and reliable in San Francisco; download the apps on your smartphone. It is advisable not to take a limousine from a taxi stand or from the street. Legally, limousines are only available for prearranged trips.

Driving

Congestion, a shortage of parking spaces, and strictly enforced laws discourage many visitors from driving in San Francisco, but possibly the best way to experience the twists and turns of Lombard Street is on four wheels.

Car Rental

For some car rental companies, you must be at least 25 years old with a valid driving license. Most agencies require a large deposit. It is slightly cheaper to rent a car from San Francisco airport. Additional rental taxes can drive up the price, especially if you hire from within the city. It is also more cost effective to do a round trip, to avoid large drop-off costs. Check your existing insurance policy before signing up to car insurance, as you may already be covered.

Rules of the Road

The maximum speed limit is 35 mph (55 km/h) in the

city. Many streets are one-way, with traffic lights at most corners. In California, if there is no oncoming traffic, drivers may turn right at a red light, always giving pedestrians the right of way. Otherwise, a red light means stop, and an amber light means proceed with caution.

Parking

Parking meters operate 9am to 6pm Monday through Saturday, except on national holidays, when parking is free. Meters in some tourist areas operate on Sundays, including at Fisherman's Wharf and the Embarcadero. Most meters have two-hour time limits, some have four-hour limits, and others no time limit at all. You can prepay from 4:30am online. Costs range from $2 to $6 per hour. City-center parking garages are also available from $16 per day.

Curbs here are color-coded. A red curb means no stopping; yellow denotes a commercial loading zone; green allows 10 to 30 minutes of parking; and white allows you to park for five minutes during business hours, with the driver remaining in the vehicle. Blue curb areas are reserved for those with disabilities. By law, you must curb your wheels when parking on steep hills. Turn your wheels into the road when your car is parked facing uphill, and toward the curb when facing down-hill. Check signs for tow warnings and follow all instructions.

Penalties

If you park your car at an out-of-order meter, expect to get a parking ticket. Blocking bus stops, fire hydrants, driveways, garages, and wheelchair ramps will also incur a fine, as will running a red light or a stop sign, or driving while texting.

Driving Outside the City

No toll payment is required to leave the city, but you will need to pay between $7 and $9.40 to re-enter. During rush hour, cars with multiple occupants can use the carpool lane, avoiding both traffic and tolls. It is legal to drive in the carpool lane when it's not rush hour, but not to avoid the bridge tolls. Those caught using the carpool lane illegally face steep fines.

Cycling

Cycling is popular in San Francisco. There are many bicycle lanes and all Muni buses are equipped to carry bikes on the outside. Bikes can also be taken on the Muni light-rail cars and on BART, although not at rush hour. There are two marked scenic bicycle routes. One goes from Golden Gate park south to Lake Merced; the other starts at the southern end of Golden Gate Bridge and crosses to Marin County.

Bicycles, equipment, and tours are available from **Bay City Bike** and **Blazing Saddles**. They rent out bikes from $8 per hour, $36 ($25 for children)

per day, or $105 for seven days. For repeated short rides, the Bay Wheels Bike Share Program is a great option.

Walking

Compact and gridded, San Francisco is entirely walkable. Downtown and the Mission, in particular, are forgivingly flat, while Nob Hill and Russian Hill reward steep climbs with spectacular views. Distances get a little more arduous once you're out on the avenues of the Richmond and Sunset, but walking is a good way to get a feel for each neighborhood.

Boats and Ferries

Ferries are one of the best ways to appreciate the beauty of the Bay Area. They shuttle to and from the cities of San Francisco, Oakland, and Larkspur, as well as the smaller towns of Tiburon and Sausalito, and nearby Angel Island. Viewing the coastline from the ferry is less expensive than a sightseeing cruise. The trip from San Francisco to Sausalito is $14.25 (children and seniors $8.50) each way and food and drink are available on board. These ferries only carry foot passengers and bicycles. **Golden Gate Ferry** and **San Francisco Bay Ferry** services depart from the Ferry Building, and the **Blue and Gold Fleet** and **Red and White Fleet** dock at Fisherman's Wharf.

Several companies also offer sightseeing cruises of the Bay. Many of these trips pass near Alcatraz,

but only **Alcatraz Cruises** stops there. **Hornblower** dining yachts offer weekend brunches and dinners from Thursday to Sunday. **Oceanic Society Expeditions** arranges nautical environmental safaris to the Farallon Islands, where whales, sea lions, seals and dolphins are often spotted. Shorter whale-watching expeditions run by **San Francisco Whale Tours** also depart from PIER 39 (check website for details).

DIRECTORY

TAXIS

Lyft
W lyft.com

Uber
W uber.com

CYCLING

Bay City Bike
W baycitybike.com

Blazing Saddles
W blazingsaddles.com

BOATS AND FERRIES

Alcatraz Cruises
W alcatrazcruises.com

Blue and Gold Fleet
W blueandgoldfleet.com

Golden Gate Ferry
W goldengate.org

Hornblower
W cityexperiences.com

Oceanic Society Expeditions
W oceanicsociety.org/expeditions

Red and White Fleet
W redandwhite.com

San Francisco Bay Ferry
W sanfranciscobayferry.com

San Francisco Whale Tours
W sanfranciscowhaletours.com

Practical Information

Passports and Visas

For entry requirements, including visas, consult your nearest US embassy or check the **US Department of State** website. Canadians typically do not require visas to enter the US, although there are some exceptions to this rule. Citizens of the UK, EU, Australia and New Zealand do not require visas if staying in the US for 90 days or less, but must apply in advance for the Electronic System for Travel Authorisation (**ESTA**). There is a small charge for this service. All other visitors need to obtain a visa in advance of traveling.

Government Advice

Now more than ever, it is important to consult both your and the US government's advice before travelling. The **US Department of State**, the **UK Foreign, Commonwealth and Development Office (FCDO)**, and the **Australian Department of Foreign Affairs and Trade** offer the latest information on security, health and local regulations.

Customs Information

You can find information on the laws relating to goods and currency taken in or out of the United States on the **US Customs and Border Protection** website. You are allowed to bring in 1.75 pints (1 liter) of wine or liquor,

200 cigarettes, 100 cigars, and $100 worth of gifts. Certain fruits and vegetables, animals, and animal products aren't allowed. You may carry up to $10,000 in US or foreign currency out of or into the country; larger sums must be declared, which entails filing the FinCEN Form 105.

Insurance

We recommend taking out a comprehensive insurance policy covering theft, loss of belongings, medical care, cancellations and delays, and read the small print carefully. The US healthcare system is predominantly private – and expensive– so it is essential to ensure medical cover.

Health

For information regarding COVID-19 vaccination requirements, consult government advice. No other inoculations are required to visit the US.

Healthcare in San Francisco is high quality but costly. Ensure you have full medical cover prior to your visit, and keep receipts to claim on your insurance if needed.

Walgreens pharmacies can be found all over the city, and branches at 498 Castro Street, 135 Powell Street, Divisadero Street, and Westborough Square are open 24 hours. Certain medications available over the counter in the UK require a prescription in the US. There are several

emergency rooms open 24 hours, including the **California Pacific Medical Center** and **Saint Francis Memorial Hospital**.

Tap water is safe to drink unless specifically stated otherwise.

Smoking, Alcohol, and Drugs

You must be over 21 to buy and drink alcohol, and to buy tobacco products. It is legal for over 21s to smoke marijuana in the home or in a building licensed for its consumption. Drinking alcohol is not allowed in most public areas, especially from open containers. Driving while under the influence of alcohol or any drug is prohibited. It is illegal to smoke in public buildings, workplaces, restaurants, and bars. It is also illegal to smoke anywhere that exposes others to second-hand smoke, including parks, beaches, and bus stops. These laws extend to e-cigarettes.

ID

Take some form of photo identification when buying alcohol, tobacco, or marijuana, as bars, clubs, restaurants, and shops are required by law to check it.

Personal Security

San Francisco is one of the safest large cities in the US. Police patrol tourist areas frequently, and few visitors are victims of street crime.

That said, it is always advisable to take the usual precautions against petty crime.

As major fault lines are found throughout the San Francisco Bay Area, earthquakes do occur from time to time. Should you experience a quake, there are simple safety guidelines to follow. If indoors, stand under a doorway or table, away from windows and wall hangings and hold on until the shaking stops. If outdoors, stay away from power cables and trees. If driving, pull over, away from power lines and bridges and remain in the car. If on the beach, move to higher ground. The Federal Emergency Management Agency (**FEMA**) has a website with useful information about safety precautions and you can also access a California-wide early warning system through the free **MyShake** app, which alerts users to earthquakes of magnitude 4.5 or higher in their area, giving them valuable seconds to prepare before any shaking starts.

As a general rule, San Franciscans are very accepting of all people, regardless of their race, gender or sexuality. California recognized the rights of those wanting to legally change their gender in the mid-1980s and same-sex marriage was legalized in 2008. San Francisco has an incredibly diverse LGBTQ+ community, with a history stretching back to the Gold Rush. The Castro district is the most welcoming area for members of the LGBTQ+ community, and information on events can be found across the city. If you do feel unsafe, the **Safe Space Alliance** pinpoints your nearest place of refuge.

For **ambulance, medical, police, and fire department** services, call the national emergency number 911 and have information on your situation and details of your location ready.

Travelers with Specific Requirements

Disabled access is extensive throughout San Francisco, from ramped curbs to telecommunication devices for hearing-impaired travelers. However, the city is famous for its steep hills, particularly around Russian Hill and Nob Hill, which may prove challenging for those with mobility issues. Public transportation is largely accessible for those with specific requirements, and prices are usually discounted. The free Muni Access Guide for public transport is available on the **SFMTA** website and **Access Northern California** provides information on accessible travel and recreation in San Francisco, the Bay Area, and beyond.

DIRECTORY

PASSPORTS AND VISAS

ESTA
[w] esta.cbp.dhs.gov

US Department of State
[w] travel.state.gov

GOVERNMENT ADVICE

Australian Department of Foreign Affairs and Trade
[w] smartraveller.gov.au

UK Foreign, Commonwealth and Development Office
[w] gov.uk/foreign-travel-advice

CUSTOMS INFORMATION

US Customs and Border Protection
[w] cbp.gov

HEALTH

California Pacific Medical Center
[w] cpmc.org

Saint Francis Memorial Hospital
[w] saintfrancismemorial.org

PERSONAL SECURITY

Ambulance, Medical, Police, and Fire Department
[c] 911

FEMA
[w] fema.gov

MyShake
[w] myshake.berkeley.edu

Safe Space Alliance
[w] safespacealliance.com

TRAVELERS WITH SPECIFIC REQUIREMENTS

Access Northern California
[w] accessnca.org

SFMTA
[w] sfmta.com

Time Difference

Contiguous US is divided into four time zones, with San Francisco in the Pacific Time Zone. It's 3 hours behind New York and 8 hours behind London. Daylight Saving Time moves the clock one hour ahead from the second Sunday in March until the first Sunday in November.

Money

The local currency is the US dollar (USD). Bank notes come in denominations of $1, $5, $10, $20, $50, and $100, while coins are 1c, 5c (nickel), 10c (dime), 25c (quarter), and the less common 50c and $1. Currency exchange is available at the three international airports, at Downtown banks and hotels, and at **Currency Exchange International**.

ATMs are the best way to get cash. To avoid the fees added to ATM transactions, make a purchase in a store and ask for cash. Debit cards are accepted for every transaction type, and many retailers now accept contactless payments.

Without a credit card, you will not be able to rent a car or check into a hotel. Visa and MasterCard are widely accepted, while Discover and Diners Club cards, or even American Express are often refused.

Electrical Appliances

The US uses 110–120 volts AC. If your appliances use 220–240 volts (as in most of Europe), bring a 110-volt transformer and a plug adapter with two flat parallel pins.

Cell Phones and Wi-Fi

Cell phone service in San Francisco is excellent. The main US network providers are AT&T, Sprint, T-Mobile US, and Verizon. Most of these offer prepaid, pay-as-you-go phones and US SIM cards, starting at around $30 (plus tax), which you can purchase upon arrival. Calls within the US are cheap, but making international calls may be pricey. Any triband or multiband cell phone should work in the US.

Wi-Fi is free at the airports and at cafés and lodgings. You can also access free Wi-Fi in public spaces by connecting to #SFWiFi. Find more hot spots at the **Open WiFi Spots** website. Computers are available to use for free at the San Francisco Visitor Information Center and libraries.

Postal Services

Most US post offices are open from 9am to 5pm Monday to Friday and from 9am to 1:30pm on Saturdays. Stamps are also available at some hotels and grocery stores. Express mail can be sent through private delivery companies, such as DHL and FedEx.

Weather

The Pacific marine climate means mild year-round weather, with temperatures seldom rising above 70° F (21° C) or falling below 40° F (5° C). Bring layers – evenings are nearly always cool, and fog can roll in any day, especially in summer.

Opening Hours

Shops are generally open daily from 10am to 5pm and often later. Some groceries, drugstores, and supermarkets are open daily from 7am to 11pm. Chain stores and malls are often open on holidays.

Banks are open from 9am to 5pm Monday to Friday, some are open on weekends. Museums and attractions have their own hours; most are open daily.

The COVID-19 pandemic proved that situations can change suddenly. Always check before visiting attractions and hospitality venues for up-to-date hours and booking requirements.

Visitor Information

The **San Francisco Visitor Information Center** is loaded with information, coupons, tour tickets, and money-saving passes for visitors. Well in advance of your arrival, check out the website with its "trip ideas" and "deals" sections, and calendar of events. You can also use it to book hotels and request a free Visitor's Guide by mail or download a digital version. At the center itself, you can pick up CityPasses, Muni passports, and maps, and make use of the Wi-Fi and computers for free.

Taking an organized trip or tour is a popular way to get around and see as much of the city and its surrounding areas as possible. The choice of such tours is plentiful. **Big Bus San Francisco** offers multilingual, hop-on-hop-off, open-top bus tours of the main attractions of the city. **San Francisco Whale Tours** sail under the Golden Gate Bridge to a vast Marine Sanctuary to see whales and sea turtles. **Alcatraz Cruises** (see p19) offer narrated ferry rides and a multilingual audio walking tour of the island. For free walking tours of the city led by savvy locals and historians, try **San Francisco City Guides**. For on-foot explorations of the Presidio, hidden stairways, urban forests, and hilly neighborhoods, **Urban Hiker San Francisco** is a good bet. **Edible Excursions** offers culinary strolls through Ferry Building Marketplace, the Mission District, and Japantown, as well as seasonal trips to West Marin. For craft beer lovers, **Bay Area Brewery Tours** shuttles people to breweries for talks and tastings.

Local Customs

San Francisco is a very laid-back city. Casual clothing is acceptable for all but the most upmarket restaurants and clubs.

Language

The official language of San Francisco is English, although more than a hundred languages are spoken across this cosmopolitan city. Spanish and Chinese are well established as second and third languages.

Taxes

Sales tax in San Francisco is 8.5 per cent. Tax is charged on everything except groceries, plants used for food, and prescription drugs, with a few other exemptions.

Accommodation

Booking a package deal including airfares and hotels (and sometimes car rentals) is often the most inexpensive way of visiting San Francisco. Make sure you book in advance to get the best deals, especially if visiting from June through August. Prices also spike around holidays and local festivals, so check your dates before you book.

The cheapest stays, especially for families, are in dormitory-style rooms in hostels (see p148); private family rooms are also available. **Hostelling International** has a good selection on its website.

Home Exchange and **Invented City** allow homeowners to trade their homes at a time convenient to both parties.

DIRECTORY

MONEY

Currency Exchange International
🆆 sanfranciscocurrency exchange.com

CELL PHONES AND WI-FI

Open WiFi Spots
🆆 openwifispots.com

VISITOR INFORMATION

Alcatraz Cruises
🆆 alcatrazcruises.com

Bay Area Brewery Tours
🆆 bayareabrewery tours.com

Big Bus San Francisco
🆆 eng.bigbustours.com

Edible Excursions
🆆 edibleexcursions.net

San Francisco City Guides
🆆 sfcityguides.org

San Francisco Visitor Information Center
MAP Q3 ▪ 900 Market St
🆆 sftravel.com

San Francisco Whale Tours
🆆 sanfranciscowhale tours.com

Urban Hiker San Francisco
🆆 urbanhikersf.com

ACCOMMODATION

Home Exchange
🆆 homeexchange.com

Hostelling International
🆆 norcalhostels.org

Invented City
🆆 invented-city.com

Places to Stay

PRICE CATEGORIES
For a standard, double room per night (with breakfast if included), taxes, and extra charges.
....
$ under $200 ■ $$ $200–$300 ■ $$$ over $300

Luxury Hotels

Cavallo Point Lodge
601 Murray Circle, Fort Baker, Sausalito ■ (888) 651-2003 ■ www.cavallo point.com ■ No air conditioning ■ $$$
A former military base, this luxury lodge has the charm of a B&B and is set in beautiful surroundings at the foot of the Golden Gate Bridge. Rooms are very comfortable and spacious.

Four Seasons
MAP P4 ■ 757 Market St ■ (415) 633-3000 ■ www. fourseasons.com ■ $$$
Designed with the business expense-account traveler in mind, this place has useful amenities such as multi-line phones and a well-run business center.

Hotel Nikko
MAP Q3 ■ 222 Mason St ■ (415) 394-1111 ■ www. hotelnikkosf.com ■ $$$
High-tech and minimalist white marble interiors radiate modernity in Hotel Nikko's Japanese-style environment. Its cool comfort and tranquil luxury, with touches such as silk wallpaper, soothe the spirit and free the mind. The Anzu restaurant is excellent. Dogs are welcomed, with dog-friendly rooms and a pet terrace.

1 Hotel San Francisco
MAP H2 ■ 8 Mission St ■ (415) 278-3700 ■ www. 1hotels.com ■ $$$
Eco-conscious and sustainable luxury reigns supreme at this urban oasis looming above the city's spectacular waterfront. Check out your preferred style of pillow in the pillow library, attend a complimentary morning yoga class or relax in one of the outdoor rooftop soaking tubs.

Hyatt Regency
MAP N6 ■ 5 Embarcadero Center ■ (415) 788-1234 ■ www.sanfrancisco regency.hyatt.com ■ $$$
The 17-story atrium lobby, one of the largest in the world, has long plants cascading down from above, a waterfall, and glass elevators. Many rooms and suites have either city or waterfront views.

JW Marriott
MAP P3 ■ 515 Mason St ■ (415) 771-8600 ■ www.marriott.com ■ $$$
It's all about location at this large, elegant hotel situated in Union Square. Rooms have all modern amenities and a 24-hour butler service. Guests rave about the pillow-top mattresses. The service is impeccable and the beautifully furnished lounge areas in the lobby are welcoming and relaxing.

Le Méridien
MAP N5 ■ 333 Battery St ■ (415) 296-2900 ■ www. starwoodhotels.com ■ $$$
Sleek and sophisticated, Le Méridien is an elegant hotel, with many of the rooms offering views over the Bay. Its restaurant, Park Grill, offers American cuisine and has a lovely patio for al fresco dining. The terrace is also a great place to enjoy drinks. The service is first-class.

Lodge at the Presidio
MAP D2 ■ 105 Montgomery St, Presidio ■ (415) 561-1234 ■ www. presidiolodging.com ■ $$$
Tucked away in the quiet Presidio, these former barracks with sweeping views of the Golden Gate have been sustainably converted into a historic hotel with modern amenities. It is the perfect retreat for families, nature lovers, and those seeking some time away from the bustling city. Complimentary shuttle rides to downtown are easily available.

Four Seasons Hotel San Francisco at Embarcadero
MAP N5 ■ 222 Sansome St ■ (415) 276-9888 ■ www.fourseasons.com/ embarcadero ■ $$$
Located on the top 11 floors of the third tallest building in Downtown, this is one of the classiest hotels you'll find in San Francisco. It offers splendid views over the Bay and city. There are also added complimentary amenities such as

free Wi-Fi, housekeeping with turndown service twice daily, and use of the house car.

Palace Hotel

MAP P5 ▪ 2 New Montgomery St ▪ (415) 512-1111 ▪ www.sf palace.com ▪ $$$

Dating from 1875, this historic landmark hotel emanates architectural splendor. The gorgeous Garden Court (where traditional afternoon tea is served) and the original Maxfield Parrish mural in the Pied Piper bar are national treasures. The rooms are wonderful and varied in terms of design, but many do not offer views.

Beacon Grand

MAP P4 ▪ 450 Powell St ▪ (415) 392-7755 ▪ www. beacongrand.com ▪ $$$

This splendid Art Deco landmark, originally known as Sir Francis Drake, is situated just a block away from Union Square. The doormen wear Beefeater costumes and the cable cars glide by constantly. The private rooms, the bistro and the two bars have a very festive feel to them.

St. Regis San Francisco

125 3rd St ▪ (415) 284-4000 ▪ www.stregis sanfrancisco.com ▪ $$$

Situated close to some of the best museums in the entire city, St. Regis is a refined and modern SoMa hotel. With a welcoming atmosphere, it features a top-rated spa, a lounge, and a restaurant. It also has an indoor infinity pool, which is quite a rarity in San Francisco.

Taj Campton Place

MAP P4 ▪ 340 Stockton St ▪ (415) 781-5555 ▪ www.tajcamptonplace. com ▪ $$$

A member of the Leading Hotels of the World and definitely one of the finest in the city, this place aims to provide personal attention to each of its guests. Expect to find the best of everything here. The restaurant, serving Californian Cuisine, also serves an elegant breakfast.

W

MAP Q5 ▪ 181 3rd St ▪ (415) 777-5300 ▪ www.wsanfrancisco. com ▪ $$$

The W Hotel unites sustainability, style, and superb service. The decor is minimalist, but with luxury touches throughout. Rooms feature flat-screen TVs and MP3 stereos. The clientele that come here for drinks are chic trendsetters, too.

The Westin St. Francis

MAP P4 ▪ 335 Powell St ▪ (415) 397-7000 ▪ www. westinstfrancis.com ▪ $$$

This grand San Francisco institution still shines in its public areas and guest rooms, which were renovated in 2018. The views from the tower rooms are phenomenal.

Boutique Hotels

Argonaut Hotel

MAP F1 ▪ 495 Jefferson St ▪ (415) 563-0800 ▪ www.argonauthotel. com ▪ $$

Featuring an exposed brick facade and waterfront views from the guest rooms, this is a pet-friendly hotel. Amenities here include free bikes to

borrow to cruise along Fisherman's Wharf, as well as six spacious rooms designated for tall people with extra-long beds and a raised shower head.

Hotel Emblem

MAP P3 ▪ 562 Sutter St ▪ (415) 433-4434 ▪ www.viceroyhotels andresorts.com ▪ $$

Steeped in the literary and artistic traditions of San Francisco, with a focus on the rebellious Beat poet spirit, this great little hotel was renovated in 2019. The guest rooms and common areas were revamped with stylish accents including a poetry projection wall. It has an on-site coffee shop, and the hotel's speakeasy-style Obscenity Bar offers classic cocktails as well as local beers on tap.

Inn at the Presidio

MAP D2 ▪ 42 Moraga Ave ▪ (415) 800-7356 ▪ www.innatthepresidio. com ▪ $$

Housed in a historic building in the heart of Presidio, close to fabulous restaurants and museums, this elegant hotel has beautiful yet simple rooms.

Petite Auberge

MAP G3 ▪ 863 Bush St ▪ (415) 928-6000 ▪ www. petiteaubergesf.com ▪ $$

Located on Nob Hill, this French Provincial-styled hotel combines the luxurious and the rustic, with brass pans hung on the walls and pillow-top mattresses on the beds. As well as the complimentary breakfast buffet, there are freshly baked cookies every afternoon.

el PRADO Hotel

520 Cowper St, Palo
Alto ▪ (650) 322-9000
▪ www.elpradopaloalto.
com ▪ $$$
The elegant, airy rooms
in this Spanish-style
hotel in downtown Palo
Alto feature private
terraces and marble
bathrooms. el PRADO
has consistently been
named one of the best
hotels in Palo Alto for
many years. Some rooms
also have fireplaces.

Enchanté Boutique Hotel

1 Main St, Los Altos
▪ (650) 946-2000
▪ www.enchantehotel.
com ▪ $$$
A favorite of Silicon
Valley visitors, this
stylish inn is modelled
on a French château.
It has luxurious
amenities, including a
library and canine con-
cierge, and offers free
breakfast, afternoon
refreshments, as well
as Wi-Fi. The charming
on-site bistro serves
dinner daily and
brunch on Sundays.

h2hotel

219 Healdsburg Ave,
Healdsburg ▪ (707) 431-
2202 ▪ www.h2hotel.
com ▪ $$$
Located in one of the
Wine Country's small
towns, h2hotel is an
environment- and
resource-conscious
hotel that features
spacious rooms, a heated
swimming pool, bikes to
borrow, and a top-notch
restaurant, Spoonbar.
An incredible breakfast
spread – which offers
homemade granola and
egg dishes to order – is
included in the room rate.

Harmon Guest House

227 Healdsburg Ave,
Healdsburg ▪ (707) 431-
8220 ▪ www.harmon
guesthouse.com ▪ $$$
This Wine Country eco-
chic boutique property
has a rooftop lounge
with a firepit. Sustainable
accents include a check-
in desk made from a
fallen eucalyptus tree.
All rooms have a patio
or balcony, and a bar cart
stocked with local spirits.
Organic breakfast is
included in the room rate.

Hotel G

MAP P3 ▪ 386 Geary St
▪ (415) 986-2000 ▪ www.
hotelgsanfrancisco.com
▪ $$$
Stay next to Union Square
in sleekly designed rooms
decorated in stylish greys
and whites with wooden
touches. The finer details
of this 1908 building have
been preserved while
adding modern comforts
to rooms like free Wi-Fi,
Smart TVs, honor bars,
and Nespresso makers.
Well-known seafood
restaurant Ayala is also
located in this hotel.

Hotel Kabuki

MAP F3 ▪ 1625 Post
St ▪ (415) 922-3200
▪ www.jdvhotels.com/
hotel-kabuki ▪ $$$
Experience Japanese
hospitality in this bou-
tique hotel in Japantown
featuring deep soaking
baths, traditional gardens
and a Zen-like ambience,
which is enhanced by the
efficient and friendly staff.

Hotel Triton

MAP P4 ▪ 342 Grant Ave
▪ (415) 394-0500 ▪ www.
hoteltriton.com ▪ $$$
Perhaps the most unique
hotel in the city, featuring
avant-garde touches such
as tarot card readings,
feather boa rental, and
several suites designed
by rock celebrities, inclu-
ding Grateful Dead's Jerry
Garcia. It's all too cool
for words; you might
run into Courtney Love
or Cher, both of whom
have stayed here.

Hotel Zephyr

MAP K3 ▪ 250 Beach St
▪ (415) 617-6555 ▪ www.
hotelzephyrsf.com ▪ $$$
A weird and wacky naval
theme (think Popeye) give
the lobby, guest rooms,
and suites a humorous
marine feel at Hotel
Zephyr. The eclectic decor
matches the waterfront
Fisherman's Wharf loca-
tion of this large, upscale
but friendly hotel.

The Inn Above Tide

30 El Portal, Sausalito
▪ (415) 332-9535 ▪ www.
innabovetide.com ▪ $$$
The only hotel built
directly on the Bay. The
views of the water from
the guest rooms' private
balconies are stunning,
and there is a serene
ambience. This is a wonder-
ful choice, convenient to
the city via the Golden Gate
Bridge or a ferry ride.

The Marker

MAP P3 ▪ 501 Geary St
▪ (415) 292-0100 ▪ www.
jdvhotels.com ▪ $$$
Situated in the heart of
the Theater District, this
quirky but extremely
comfortable hotel is run
to perfection. The fairy-
tale decor is joyously
original, being at once a
celebration of color and
elegance, and the beds
are perhaps the most
comfortable in the world.
The stylish restaurant is

an attraction in itself, with polished oak and brass ornaments.

Mill Valley Inn
165 Throckmorton Ave, Mill Valley ■ (415) 389-6608 ■ www.millvalley inn.com ■ $$$
Blending the sophistication of a European hotel – tea is served all day – with the charm of a Californian mill town, this intimate option is tucked away in a redwood grove.

Hilltop Hotels

Hotel Sausalito
16 El Portal at Bridgeway, Sausalito ■ (415) 332-0700 ■ www.hotel sausalito.com ■ $$
With a quirky back story, this boutique hotel has sixteen luxurious rooms, with custom furnishings, and suites decorated in pastel hues that offer park and harbor views.

Queen Anne Hotel
MAP F3 ■ 1590 Sutter at Octavia ■ (415) 441-2828 ■ www.queenanne. com ■ $$
Built in 1890, this old mansion has been lovingly refurbished according to Victorian taste. The rooms are individually decorated and filled with antiques. The continental breakfast is complimentary, and the morning newspaper too.

Claremont Hotel Club & Spa
41 Tunnel Rd, Berkeley ■ (510) 843-3000 ■ www. fairmont.com/claremont-berkeley ■ $$$
This country club-style resort in the Berkeley Hills was built in 1915 and still retains the feel of that

era. There are business services, a fitness center, two pools, tennis courts, and views of the Golden Gate Bridge.

Fairmont
MAP N3 ■ 950 Mason St ■ (415) 772-5000 ■ www. fairmont.com ■ $$$
"Opulent" and "palatial" barely begin to describe this *grande dame* of San Francisco's hotels, taking pride of place on Nob Hill. The rooms and service are commensurate with its superior status.

Hotel Drisco
MAP E2 ■ 2901 Pacific Ave ■ (415) 346-2880 ■ www. hoteldrisco.com ■ $$$
This Pacific Heights property has won many top hotel awards through the years, and, although the elegance is perhaps a little understated, it delivers on service. Details include complimentary continental breakfast, as well as some of the very best vistas San Francisco has to offer.

InterContinental Mark Hopkins
MAP N3 ■ 999 California St ■ (415) 392-3434 ■ www.sfmarkhopkins. com ■ $$$
The top-notch restaurant here is a major pull, with its 360-degree panoramic views of the city, and the service is genuinely caring. The rooms are provided with every amenity and achieve an excellent standard of comfort.

Laurel Inn
MAP E3 ■ 444 Presidio Ave ■ (415) 567-8467 ■ www.hyatt.com ■ $$$
This stylish hotel is located in Presidio Heights, and

is decorated in a hip mid-century fashion. Some rooms feature kitchenettes, and they all come equipped with flat-screen TVs and Blu-Ray players. Breakfast, daily newspapers and refreshments in the lobby are included.

The Ritz-Carlton
MAP N4 ■ 600 Stockton St ■ (415) 296-7465 ■ www.ritzcarlton.com ■ $$$
Experience the ultimate in luxury and service at this hotel. Views from the rooms are magnificent, the staff are at the top of their game, and the food is nothing short of sublime.

The Scarlet Huntington
MAP N3 ■ 1075 California St ■ (415) 474-5400 ■ www.thescarlethotels. com ■ $$$
Situated at the top of Nob Hill, across from Grace Cathedral, this hotel feels like the clubby apartment of a rich uncle with impeccable taste. The rooms are luxurious and there's an excellent restaurant, plus a spa where you can indulge in a caviar facial.

Stanford Court
MAP N3 ■ 905 California St ■ (415) 989-3500 ■ www.stanfordcourt. com ■ $$$
Long a business favorite, this hotel is situated near the top of Nob Hill, close to almost everything Downtown. The stained-glass dome in the lobby gives it a grand feel. It is eco- and pet-friendly, and offers complimentary Wi-Fi and free bicycles for visitors.

For a key to hotel price categories see p142

LGBTQ+ friendly Hotels

Hotel Zeppelin

MAP G4 ■ 545 Post St ■ (415) 563-0303 ■ www. zhotelssf.com ■ No air conditioning ■ $

This hotel in the Lower Nob Hill neighborhood is known for its modern touches, industrial bar, and for hosting the occasional drag bingo night. One of the city's foremost LGBTQ+-friendly hotels, it is located just a few blocks away from the downtown shopping area, as well as the gastronomic delights of the nearby Tenderloin district. The stylish rooms truly celebrate the city's rambunctious nature.

The Axiom Hotel

MAP N4 ■ 28 Cyril Magnin St ■ (415) 392-9466 ■ $$

Set next to the Powell-Hyde cable car, this charming pet-friendly hotel combines architectural details of the 1900s with green initiatives and technological conveniences. There are meeting rooms and a fitness center.

Beck's Motor Lodge

MAP F4 ■ 2222 Market St ■ (415) 621-8212 ■ www. becksmotorlodge.com ■ $$

Basic but modern rooms are on offer in this renovated no-smoking lodge with a private sun deck, as well as free parking and Wi-Fi. Situated in a lively area of the city, it is especially popular with LGBTQ+ people.

Chateau Tivoli

MAP E3 ■ 1057 Steiner St ■ (415) 776-5462 ■ www. chateautivoli.com ■ No air conditioning ■ $$

The rooms and suites in this stunning old building are named after Mark Twain, Enrico Caruso, Jack London, and other notable personalities, to remind guests of San Francisco's illustrious history. Rooms have four-poster beds and feature decorative fireplaces and bay windows.

The Inn San Francisco

MAP F5 ■ 943 South Van Ness Ave ■ (415) 641-0188 ■ www. innsf.com ■ No air conditioning ■ $$

This fine Victorian mansion serves a buffet breakfast in its charming parlors. The garden has a redwood hot tub, plus a sundeck with a panoramic view of the city.

The Parker Guest House

MAP F5 ■ 520 Church St ■ (415) 621-3222 ■ www. parkerguesthouse.com ■ No air conditioning ■ $$

An Edwardian mini-mansion, located just steps away from various gay bars and restaurants, this guesthouse has expansive gardens and sun decks.

Virgin Hotel

MAP G3 ■ 250 4th St ■ (415) 534-6500 ■ $$$

This trendy SoMa district Virgin property welcomes all. Amenities at this pet-friendly hotel include a fitness center and a huge rooftop bar on the 12th floor, called Everdene.

Neighborhood Hotels

Pacific Heights Inn

MAP F2 ■ 1555 Union St ■ (415) 776-3310 ■ www.pacificheights innsf.com ■ No air conditioning ■ $

Set on a quiet block close to public transport links, this motel offers basic but comfortable rooms. There is free on-site parking, Wi-Fi, and a continental breakfast. Some rooms also feature kitchens.

Seal Rock Inn

MAP A3 ■ 545 Point Lobos Ave ■ (415) 752-8000 ■ www.sealrock inn.com ■ $

This inn is in a handy location for visiting Cliff House and Land's End (see p117), as well as the Legion of Honor. Rooms are large, though plain, and there's a sun deck, table tennis, and a pool for the summer months. Free parking is available.

Hotel Zetta

MAP G3 ■ 55 Fifth Street ■ (415) 543-8555 ■ $$

In the heart of downtown just off of Market Street, this hotel is perfect for a sociable stay. It comes with a games room and there is also a fitness center, a meeting room, and a stylish dining area.

Hotel Del Sol

MAP E2 ■ 3100 Webster St ■ (415) 921-5520 ■ www.jdvhotels.com ■ $$

Described as "festive and spacious," this boutique hotel is a ray of sunshine. Bright colors and cheerful patterns greet you around every corner, and the staff are just as nice as can be. This is an especially great place to stay if you are traveling with kids.

Marina Motel

MAP E2 ▪ 2576 Lombard St ▪ (415) 921-3430 ▪ www.marinamotel. com ▪ $$

Tucked away in a flowery Mediterranean courtyard decorated with murals, this motel offers guests a peaceful oasis right in the heart of the Marina District, close to restaurants and public transport links. Rooms are simple and clean, and parking is included.

Metro Hotel

MAP E4 ▪ 319 Divisadero St ▪ (415) 861-5364 ▪ www.metrohotelsf. com ▪ $$

This conveniently located, family-owned boutique hotel is housed in a vintage Victorian walk-up (there are no elevators). The comfortable rooms are minimalist and all have private bathrooms. Guests can relax in the lush private garden.

Stanyan Park Hotel

MAP D4 ▪ 750 Stanyan St ▪ (415) 751-1000 ▪ www.stanyanpark.com ▪ No air conditioning ▪ $$

Listed on the National Register of Historic Places, this Victorian hotel has been receiving guests since 1904. It is located right on Golden Gate Park and is decorated in period style. The hotel is known for its generous continental breakfast spread, along with free Wi-Fi, and a front desk that operates around the clock.

Jackson Court

MAP F2 ▪ 2198 Jackson St ▪ (415) 929-7670 ▪ www. jacksoncourt.com ▪ $$$

Located in the Pacific Heights area, this is a magnificent 1900 brownstone mansion. The wood-paneled parlor is an inviting place, and the stone fireplace provides warmth to enjoy afternoon tea.

Phoenix Hotel

MAP Q2 ▪ 601 Eddy St ▪ (415) 776-1380 ▪ www. jdvhotels.com ▪ $$$

Johnny Depp and the late John F. Kennedy Jr have all stayed in this retro-style motorlodge, with a courtyard pool. Despite the glitzy clientele, it is located close to the gritty Tenderloin area, which is only for the most self-assured. Continental breakfast is included and the restaurant/bar attracts trendy crowds.

Marriot Vacation Club Pulse

MAP K3 ▪ 2620 Jones St ▪ (415) 885-4700 ▪ www. pier2620hotel.com ▪ $$$

Located in the buzzing Fisherman's Wharf area, a short walk from Pier 39, and with many shops and restaurants on the street, this hotel offers comfy rooms. Street noise can be an issue, so ask for a room facing the courtyard if you are a light sleeper.

B&Bs and Guesthouses

Hayes Valley Inn

MAP F3 ▪ 417 Gough St ▪ (415) 862-9051 ▪ www. hayesvalleyinn.com ▪ $

A budget B&B option, but with a certain charm. The basic rooms have shared bathrooms.

Cliff Crest Inn B&B

407 Cliff St, Santa Cruz ▪ (831) 427-2609 ▪ www. cliffcrestinn.com ▪ No air conditioning ▪ $$

Surrounded by redwoods, the rooms in this Queen Anne Victorian are graced with fresh flowers, and some also have views over the Bay.

Gables Inn

62 Princess St, Sausalito ▪ (415) 289-1100 ▪ www.gablesinn sausalito.com ▪ No air conditioning ▪ $$

A luxurious, 14-room B&B with gorgeous Bay views, this hotel is the perfect spot for a romantic break. Suites are also available.

Golden Gate Hotel

MAP B4 ▪ 775 Bush St ▪ (415) 392-3702 ▪ www. goldengatehotel.com ▪ $$

Combining Edwardian charm with modern amenities, this hotel is one of the best small guesthouses within the city. It is family-run, with small, but luxurious, rooms. Tea and freshly baked cookies are available every afternoon.

Monte Cristo Bed and Breakfast

MAP E3 ▪ 600 Presidio Ave ▪ (888) 666-1875 ▪ www.bedandbreakfastsf.com ▪ No air conditioning ▪ $$

Conveniently located in the Pacific Heights neighborhood – just a short walk to The Presidio park (see p56) – this quaint hotel features Edwardian-era decor, which transports you to the early 20th century.

For a key to hotel price categories see p142

Mountain Home Inn
810 Panoramic Hwy, Mill Valley ▪ **(415) 381-9000** ▪ **www.mtnhomeinn.com** ▪ **$$**

Step out of the door of this quaint mountainside inn and be blown away by the spectacular views it has of San Francisco Bay and Mount Tamalpais. Situated just 20 minutes from Downtown, this hikers' paradise invites you to meander to the beachside town of Stinson or to historic Muir Woods. Afterward, indulge in a hearty gourmet meal.

The Pelican Inn
10 Pacific Way, Muir Beach ▪ **(415) 383-6000** ▪ **www.pelicaninn.com** ▪ **No air conditioning** ▪ **$$**

Majestically positioned deep in a valley, each of the seven rooms has antiques, and a roaring fire is lit every day in the inglenook fireplace.

The Union Street Inn
MAP E2 ▪ **2229 Union St** ▪ **(415) 346-0424** ▪ **www.unionstreetinn.com** ▪ **$$**

Combining the elegance and gentility of a grand Edwardian home, this inn is located just up from the Marina and right on fashionable Union Street. The individually decorated rooms are all spacious, with original antiques and art, fine linens, fresh flowers, and complimentary chocolates and fruit.

White Swan Inn
MAP N3 ▪ **845 Bush St** ▪ **(415) 775-1755** ▪ **www.whiteswaninnsf.com** ▪ **$$**

This quaint B&B in the heart of Downtown resembles a country inn, with bright floral prints,

Victorian-style canopied beds, and cozy fireplaces. An evening wine reception and English breakfast are both complimentary.

Budget Hotels

Coventry Inn
MAP F2 ▪ **1901 Lombard St** ▪ **(415) 567-1200** ▪ **www.coventrymotorinn.com** ▪ **$**

A good, basic motel, offering large, pleasant rooms with bay windows, located on the Marina's "Motel Row." It offers functional and reliable accommodation along with complimentary Wi-Fi and parking. A minimum stay may apply on some weekends.

Hostelling International Downtown
MAP P3 ▪ **312 Mason St** ▪ **(415) 788-5604** ▪ **www.hiusa.org** ▪ **No en-suite bathrooms** ▪ **No air conditioning** ▪ **$**

This location acts as the perfect base for all the major sights. Rooms hold up to five beds. All major public transportation is just outside and there's lots of tourist information available, too.

Hostelling International Fisherman's Wharf
MAP F1 ▪ **Fort Mason, Building 240** ▪ **(415) 771-7277** ▪ **www.hihostels.com/hostels/hi-san-francisco-fishermans-wharf** ▪ **$**

This hostel offers free breakfast, Wi-Fi, and parking. It's just a short walk to everything along the Bayshore. It is surrounded by a

National Park on one side and provides breathtaking views of the Bay.

Inn at the Opera
MAP F3 ▪ **333 Fulton St** ▪ **(415) 863-8400** ▪ **www.shellhospitality.com** ▪ **No air conditioning** ▪ **$**

These 48 studios and suites are walking distance from the War Memorial Opera House Civic Center, City Hall, and the Louise M. Davies Symphony Hall. Each apartment offers a kitchenette, free breakfast, and Wi-Fi. There is also an on-site café and bar.

Inn on Broadway
MAP E3 ▪ **2201 Van Ness Ave** ▪ **(415) 776-7900** ▪ **www.broadwaymanor.com** ▪ **$**

All rooms at this inn feature flat-screen TVs, and coffee- and tea-making facilities. Smoking is prohibited and there is free parking and Wi-Fi. The location is an added advantage, as many of San Francisco's eye catching sites are within walking distance from the inn.

Samesun San Francisco
M1 ▪ **1475 Lombard St** ▪ **(415) 441-6000** ▪ **www.samesun.com** ▪ **$**

A convenient location and clean, cheerful ambience make these shared bunk rooms or simple en-suite private rooms an excellent budget choice.

San Francisco Zen Center
MAP F4 ▪ **300 Page St** ▪ **(415) 863-3136** ▪ **www.sfzc.org** ▪ **No en-suite bathrooms** ▪ **No air conditioning** ▪ **$**

The Zen Center offers several comfortable,

quiet rooms available for those who are interested in learning more about Zen practices and Buddhist techniques of meditation.

The Cartwright Hotel
MAP B4 ■ 524 Sutter St ■ (415) 421-2865 ■ www.cartwrightunionsquare.com ■ $$

This pet-friendly hotel has a fireplace in the lobby, simple rooms, and free Wi-Fi. It also has a great location, very close to the Theater District.

Cow Hollow Inn and Suites
MAP E2 ■ 2190 Lombard St ■ (415) 921-5800 ■ www.cowhollowmotorinn.com ■ $$

Larger-than-average rooms, with floral wallpaper and traditional furniture and a homey feel. Some suites have Beautiful carpets accenting wood floors, marble fireplaces, and antiques.

Hotel Griffon
MAP H2 ■ 155 Steuart St ■ (415) 495-2100 ■ www.hotelgriffon.com ■ $$

Situated right on the Embarcadero near the Ferry Building, this European-style hotel has 62 rooms. Perry's restaurant and bar serves American comfort food. Free Wi-Fi available.

The Mosser
MAP Q4 ■ 54 4th St ■ (415) 986-4400 ■ www.themosser.com ■ No air conditioning ■ $$

It's hard to beat this location, less than a block from the center of Market Street and the nearest subway station. The

Mosser has a few other things going for it as well – clean rooms with Ikea furnishings, great prices, and free morning coffee, tea, and muffins in the lobby.

San Remo Hotel
MAP K3 ■ 2237 Mason St ■ (415) 776-8688 ■ www.sanremohotel.com ■ No en-suite bathrooms ■ No air conditioning ■ $$

North Beach's biggest bargain is full of charms. Each room is decorated with antiques, and the corridors feature brass railings and hanging plants under skylights. Every room has its own sink, while the other bathroom facilities can be found down the hall.

Apartments and Private Homes

Fairmont Heritage Place – Ghirardelli Square
MAP F1 ■ 900 North Point St ■ (415) 268-9900 ■ $$$

These luxurious apartments with exposed brick walls, fireplaces, and beautiful views are equipped with full kitchens and laundry facilities. The many available services include private chefs, child care, grocery delivery, and in-suite massage.

The Gateway
MAP N6 ■ 460 Davis Court ■ (833) 682-0254 ■ www.thegateway.com ■ $

Location is everything at these fully furnished, apartments, which are just steps away from a host of retail stores, restaurants, and local transportation options.

Offering every amenity and service one could possibly want when planning a long visit, these apartments promise a convenient and comfortable stay.

Monroe Residence Club
MAP N1 ■ 1870 Sacramento St ■ (415) 474-6200 ■ www.monroeresidenceclub.com ■ No air conditioning ■ $

Located amid the grand mansions of Pacific Heights, the Monroe combines the best elements of a hotel and an apartment. American-style breakfasts and four-course dinners are included. Maid service is also provided.

Noe's Nest
MAP F5 ■ 1257 Guerrero St ■ (415) 821-0751 ■ $$

The charming rooms in this ornate restored Victorian home have their own distinctive characters. Amenities include kitchenettes and spa tubs, and guests have access to a full kitchen, a garden patio, and a balcony. Full buffet breakfast available. Pets are welcome (extra fee).

The Suites at Fisherman's Wharf
MAP F1 ■ 2655 Hyde St ■ (415) 771-0200 ■ www.extraholidays.com ■ $$

An easy walk to Fisherman's Wharf and public transport, this apartment hotel offers 24 one- and two-bedroom suites with amenities that include kitchenettes, dining and living areas, and balconies.

For a key to hotel price categories see p142

General Index

Stanford University 83, 126

Stein, Gertrude 125

Steinbeck, John 82

Sterling Vineyard 36

Stern, Sigmund 118

Stern Grove Festival 81

Stinson Beach 58, 126–7

Stockton Street Chinese Markets 23

Stores *see* Shopping

Stow Lake 7, 24

Strauss, Joseph 12, 13

Streetcars 135

Stroud, Robert 20

Strybing Arboretum and Botanical Garden 24

Summer of Love (1967) 43, 104

Sundance Saloon 71

Sunset District 118–19

Sutro, Adolph 117

Sutro Baths 118, 119

Sutter, John 42

Swimming 60

Synagogues

    Congregation Sherith Israel 47

T

Tartine Bakery and Café 74, 115

Taxes 141

Taxis 136

Telegraph Hill 89, 90

Telephones 140

Temples

    Chinatown 23

    Kong Chow Temple 47

    Temple Emanu El 47

    Tin How Temple 5, 7, 23, 47, 62

    Vedanta Temple 47

Tenderloin Museum 51

Tennis 60

Tet Festival 81

Theater 66–7

The Three Shades (Rodin) 50

Tiburon 127

Time difference 140

Tin How Temple 5, 7, 23, 47, 62

The Tonga Room and Hurricane Bar 48, 68, 92

Traditional hotels 143–4

Trains 134, 135

    Napa Valley train 36

Transamerica Pyramid 48

Transport tickets 135

Travel 134–7

Travel insurance 138

Travelers with specific requirements 139

Treasure Island 96

Trestle 72, 95

Tribal, Folk & Textile Arts Show 81

Trips and tours 140–41

Twin Peaks 71, 111

U

Union Square 6, 7, 77, 89

Union Street 77, 103

Universities 126

Upper Fillmore Street 77

Upper Grant 89, 90

V

Vaccinations 138

Vedanta Temple 47

Vesuvio Café 75, 90

Visas 138, 139

Visitor information 140–41

W

Walking 79, 137

    see also Hiking

Walt Disney Family Museum 51

War Memorial Opera House 44, 66

Washington Square 89, 90

Waterfront ramble 78

Wathernam, Frank 20

Weather 140

Wells Fargo History Museum 51

Western Addition 105

Westfield San Francisco Centre 77

Wharf Area shops 100

White, Dan 43

Wi-Fi 140

Wild Side West 71

Wilkes Bashford 76

Williams, Robin 54, 118

Winchester Mystery House 128

Windmill, Dutch 7, 24

Windsurfing 61

Wine 37

Wine Country 5, 11, **36–9**

    day trips 7, 83

    spas 38–9

Women's Building 49

Woodside 128

Wright, Frank Lloyd 48

Writers 54–5

Wave Organ 47

Y

Yerba Buena Center 110

Yerba Buena Center for the Arts Theater 34

Yerba Buena Gardens 6, 7, **34–5**, 57

Yountville 7, 36

Z

Zen Center 46

Zoos

    Randall Museum 64

    San Francisco Zoo 64, 119

Acknowledgments

This edition updated by

Contributor Amber Charmei
Senior Editor Dipika Dasgupta, Alison McGill
Senior Designer Stuti Tiwari
Project Editor Alex Pathe
Assistant Editor Tavleen Kaur
Assistant Art Editor Divyanshi Shreyaskar
Picture Research Administrator Vagisha Pushp
Manager Picture Research Taiyaba Khatoon
Publishing Assistant Halima Mohammed
Jacket Designer Jordan Lambley
Cartographer Ashif
Cartography Manager Suresh Kumar
DTP Designer Rohit Rojal
Senior Production Editor Jason Little
Production Controller Kariss Ainsworth
Managing Editors Shikha Kulkarni,
Beverly Smart, Hollie Teague
Managing Art Editor Sarah Snelling
Senior Managing Art Editor Priyanka Thakur
Art Director Maxine Pedliham
Publishing Director Georgina Dee

DK would like to thank the following for their
contribution to the previous editions: Hilary Bird,
Sam Cook, Lauren Viera.

The publisher would like to thank the following for
their kind permission to reproduce their photographs:

(**Key:** a-above; b-below/bottom; c-centre; f-far; l-left;
r-right; t-top)

111 Minna Gallery: 53cla.

4Corners: SIME/Maurizio Rellini 14–5c; Susanne
Kremer 120–1.

Alamy Stock Photo: Shiiko Alexander 91tl;
Mark Bassett 48cl; Nancy Hoyt Belcher 26cl; J
an Butchofsky 25cra; Felix Choo 88b;
DanitaDelimont.com/Chuck Haney 51tr; Danita
Delimont 62t; Directphoto Collection 75bl, 76br;
Randy Duchaine 18cr; Dianne Feinstein statue by
Lisa Reinertson 43bc; Enlightened Images/Gary
Crabbe 119cl; Granger Historical Picture Archive,
NYC 42br; Seth Grant 14bl; Michael Halberstadt
104bl; Dave G. Houser 63cla; Matthew Kiernan
93bl; Bob Kreisel 61cra; Jackie Link 44bc; Stefano
Politi Markovina 4crb; Mountain Light/Galen
Rowell 12br; Eric Nathan 23clb; Nikreates 66t,
67cl, 78t; Old Books Images 88cla; Wiliam Perry
35bl; PhotoBliss 116tl; PhoodFotog 73tr; Robert
Rosenblum 27cr; Leonid Serebrennikov 90br;
Stars and Stripes 82b; travelpix 68br; UPI/
Mohammad Kheirkhah 81tr; ZUMA Press,
Inc 27tr, 55tr.

Asian Art Museum: Orange Photography 50b.

AWL Images: Stefano Politi Markovina 4t.

Blue Bottle Cafe: Claypix.com/Clay McLachlan 74bl.

California Academy of Sciences: Tim Griffith 26br;
Chris Picon 27tl.

The Chapel: Hardy Wilson 113cr.

Corbis: Morton Beebe 23tl; Gerald French 90–1;
Historical 45tr; Masterfile/Jose Luis Stephens 32tl;
Proehl Studios/Steve Proehl 2tl, 8–9, Mural in the
Beach Chalet at Ocean Beach by artist, Lucien
Labaudt 49br; San Francisco Chronicle 13tl; Phil
Schermeister 47tr; Sunset Boulevard 20crb.

de Young Museum: 29bl; Gregory Bertolini 28–9c;
Painting of Boatmen on the Missouri George Caleb
Bingham 29tl; Henrik Kam 28cla.

Delfina Restaurant: Eric Wolfinger 115b.

Dorling Kindersley Ltd: Courtesy of Grace Cathedral
87br; Jack London statue by Cedric Wentworth 54c;
Willie Mays statue by William Behrends at AT&T
Park 109tc; Courtesy of the Natural History
Museum, London/Tim Parmenter 129cb.

Dreamstime.com: Allard1 21tr; Brandon Bourdages
80cla; Canbalci 10–1t; Chee-onn Leong 59t; Cminor
58b; Kobby Dagan 80br; Drserg 50tr; David Edelman
43tr; Efeah0 17cr; F8grapher 19cr; Filiola 11tr;
Friday 128tr; Gmargittai 25bc; Diego Grandi 16–7c;
Hviola 60tl; Issalina 12bl; Jabiru 18ca; Jerryway
62cr; Jetjock 24–5c; Jewhyte 11cr; Jiawangkun
88cb; Scott Jones 89tl; Jpldesigns 46tl; Kazmaniac
36–7c; Russell Linton 11ca; Luckydoor
96tl; Lunamarina 7br, 103t; Lyngbyvej 19cl;
Maciejbledowski 18–9b; Martinmolcan 12–3c, 110bl;
Masterlu 109br; Meinzahn 17clb; Michaelurmann
4bl; MNStudio 82tl; Eli Mordechai 60bl; Sean
Pavone 48br; William Perry 46br; Photoquest 24bl;
Povalec 10bc; Qweszxcj 6tr; Radekdrewek 16clb;
Rahurlburt 34cl; Rfoxphoto 34bc; Robynmac 75tr;
Romrodinka 5clb; Valerio Rosati 106tl; Sborisov 3tr,
10cl, 132–3; Spvvkr 126t; Srongkrod 78br; Tasstock
104tr; Pamela Tekiel 18clb; David Tran 65tr;
Ronniechua 10clb; Rudy Umans 32t; Un-
fetteredmind 125t; Vampy1 92t; Ventdusud
105cl; Vitalyedush 4cra; Vonshots 4cla; Walleyelj
4br, 16br; Wizreist 18tr; Wolterk 97t; Zhukovsky
Sphinx statue by Arthur Putnam 28c, 36bl.

Exploratorium, www.exploratorium.edu: Gayle
Laird 65clb.

The Fairmont, San Francisco: 68t.

The Fairmont Sonoma Mission Inn & Spa: 38cl.

Courtesy of Fraenkel Gallery, San Francisco: 52bl.

Gayle's Bakery: Gayle's Bakery 131tr.

Getty Images: AFP / JOSH EDELSON 81cl; Archive
Photos / Buyenlarge 42t; Richard Cummins 64t;
De Agostini Picture Library 108tl; FilmMagic /
Kelly Sullivan 69tr; Glow Images, Jeff Hahne 66bc;
Inc 86tl; The Image Bank / Jim Smithson 1; The
LIFE Picture Collection/Ralph Crane 21bl; Tim
Mosenfelder 79tr; Movie Poster Image Art 13bc;
Radius Images 118b; Redferns/Daniel Boczarski
55cl; George Rose 34–35; San Francisco Chronicle /
Hearst Newspapers / Yalonda M. James 70b;
Ezra Shaw 61tr; Sports Studio Photos 55bl; The
Washington Post/John Cohen 54tl; WIN-Initiative
Labyrinth artwork by Eduardo Aguilera formed of
rocks overlooking ocean 117b; www.35mmNegative.
com 98t; Barry Winiker 15tl.

The Hess Collection: 11crb, 37cr.

iStockphoto.com: coleong 56cr.

Jackson & Polk: 100bl.

Meritage Resort and Spa: Rex Gelert 39cla.

Oakland Museum of California: 129cra.

Outerlands: Eric Wolfinger 123tr.

Paul's Hat Works: 122bl.

Paxton Gate: 112br.

Powell's Sweet Shoppe: 130c.

Presidio Trust: 56b.

Quince: 93ca; Patrik Argast 72t.

Rex Features: 20tl.

Robert Harding Picture Library: Richard Cummins 34–5c, 99cl; Juergen Richter 36cl; P. Schickert 2tr, 40–1; Marco Simoni 22bl.

San Francisco Museum Of Modern Art: Snøhetta expansion of the new SFMOMA, 2016; photo: © Henrik Kam, courtesy SFMOMA / Henrik Kam 32b, 110–111b.

Shady Lane: 130bl.

Shutterstock.com: lv-olga 27br.

Silverado Resort and Spa: Joann Dost 39b.

Spruce: 73bl.

St. John Coltrane African Orthodox Church: 47cla.

Tacolicious: Aubrie Pick 101tr.

Tartine Bakery & Cafe: OpenKitchenPhotography/ Eric Wolfinger 74tr.

Tatiana Bilbao ESTUDIO: Steve Hall 33bc.

Yerba Buena Gardens: 57tr.

Cover

Front and spine: **Getty Images:** The Image Bank / Jim Smithson.

Back: **Alamy Stock Photo:** Maciej Bledowski tl, lucky-photographer cla, Sergey Novikov crb; **Getty Images:** The Image Bank / Jim Smithson b; **iStockphoto.com:** NAN104 btr.

Pull out map cover

Getty Images: The Image Bank / Jim Smithson.

All other images are: © Dorling Kindersley.
For further information see: www.dkimages.com

Illustrator chrisorr.com

First edition created by Sargasso Media Ltd, London

Penguin Random House

First edition 2003

First published in Great Britain by Dorling Kindersley Limited DK, One Embassy Gardens, 8 Viaduct Gardens, London, SW11 7BW, UK

The authorised representative in the EEA is Dorling Kindersley Verlag GmbH. Arnulfstr. 124, 80636 Munich, Germany

Published in the United States by DK Publishing, 1745 Broadway, 20th Floor, New York, NY 10019, USA

Copyright © 2003, 2023 Dorling Kindersley Limited

A Penguin Random House Company

23 24 25 26 10 9 8 7 6 5 4 3 2 1

All rights reserved.

No part of this publication may be reproduced, stored in or introduced into a retrieval system, or transmitted in any form, or by any means (electronic, mechanical, photocopying, recording or otherwise) without the prior written permission of the copyright owner.

The publishers cannot accept responsibility for any consequences arising from the use of this book, nor for any material on third party websites, and cannot guarantee that any website address in this book will be a suitable source of travel information.

A CIP catalog record is available from the British Library.

A catalog record for this book is available from the Library of Congress.

ISSN 1479-344X

ISBN 978-0-2416-2126-4

Printed and bound in Malaysia

www.dk.com

As a guide to abbreviations in visitor information blocks: **Adm** = *admission charge;* **L** = *lunch;* **D** = *dinner.*

MIX
Paper from responsible sources
FSC™ C018179

This book was made with Forest Stewardship Council™ certified paper – one small step in DK's commitment to a sustainable future.
For more information go to www.dk.com/our-green-pledge

Street Index